Mighty in Power

The Miracles of Jesus

Mighty in Power
The Miracles of Jesus

Jeanne Kun

the WORD
among us®
press

Copyright © 2006 by The Word Among Us Press.

The Word Among Us Press
9639 Doctor Perry Road
Ijamsville, Maryland 21754
www.wordamongus.org

ISBN 13: 978-1 59325-083-6

Made and printed in the United States of America.
11 10 09 08   2 3 4 5

Cover and text design: David Crosson

Nihil Obstat: The Reverend Michael Morgan, Chancellor
                  Censor Librorum
                  May 26, 2006
Imprimatur: +Most Reverend Victor Galeone
                  Bishop of St. Augustine
                  May 26, 2006

Library of Congress Cataloging-in-Publication Data

Kun, Jeanne, 1951-
  Mighty in power : the miracles of Jesus / Jeanne Kun.
     p. cm. -- (The Word Among Us keys to the Bible)
  Includes bibliographical references.
  ISBN-13: 978-1-59325-083-6 (alk. paper)
  ISBN-10: 1-59325-083-5 (alk. paper)
  1. Jesus Christ--Miracles--Textbooks. I. Title. II. Series.
  BT366.3.K86 2006
  226.7'06--dc22
                            2006015006

Contents

Welcome to
The Word Among Us
Keys to the Bible

Have you ever lost your keys? Everyone seems to have at least one "lost keys" story to tell. Maybe you had to break a window of your house or wait for the auto club to let you into your car. Whatever you had to do probably cost you—in time, energy, money, or all three. Keys are definitely important items to have on hand!

The guides in The Word Among Us Keys to the Bible series are meant to provide you with a handy set of keys that can "unlock" the treasures of the Scriptures for you. Scripture is God's living word. Within its pages we meet the Lord. So as we study and meditate on Scripture and unlock its many treasures, we discover the riches it contains—and in the process, we grow in intimacy with God.

Since 1982, *The Word Among Us* magazine has helped Catholics develop a deeper relationship with the Lord through daily meditations that bring the Scriptures to life. More than ever, Catholics today desire to read and pray with the Scriptures, and many have begun to form small faith-sharing groups to explore the Bible together.

We recently conducted a survey among our magazine readers to learn what they wanted in a Catholic Bible study. The many enthusiastic responses we received led us to create this new series. Readers told us they are looking for easy-to-understand, faith-filled materials that approach Scripture from a clearly Catholic perspective. Moreover, they want a Bible study that shows them how they can apply what they learn from Scripture to their everyday lives. And since most of our readers lead busy lives, they asked for sessions that they can complete in an hour or two.

On the basis of the survey results, we set out to design a simple, easy-to-use Bible study guide that is also challenging and thought provoking. We hope that this guide fulfills those admittedly ambitious goals. We are confident, however, that taking the time to go through this guide—whether by yourself, with a friend, or in a small group—will be a worthwhile endeavor that will bear fruit in your life.

Sometimes the riches contained in the Old and New Testament can seem inaccessible, but we only need the right "key" to unlock them. In *Mighty in Power: The Miracles of Jesus,* we will unlock some of the gospel accounts of Jesus' miracles. Exploring these miracles can give us valuable insights into Jesus' own heart and his mission of salvation—insights that will move us to a greater faith in him, in his love for us, and in his saving power.

How to Use the Guides in This Series

The study guides in the Keys to the Bible series are divided into six sessions that each deal with a particular aspect of the topic. Before starting the first session, take the time to read the introduction, which contains helpful background information on the Scripture texts to be studied. It will provide the foundation for the six sessions that follow. In this guide, the introduction examines the meaning of Jesus' miracles and their place in his mission and ministry, while each session focuses on a specific miracle that Jesus performed.

Whether you use this guide for personal reflection and study, as part of a faith-sharing group, or as an aid in your prayer time, be sure to begin each session with prayer. Ask God to open his word to you and to speak to you personally. Read each Scripture passage slowly and carefully. Then, take as much time as you need to meditate on the passage and pursue any thoughts it brings to mind. When you are ready, move on to the accompanying commentary, which offers various insights into the text.

Two sets of questions are included in each session to help you "mine" the Scripture passage and discover its relevance to your life. Those under the heading "Understand!" focus on the text itself and help you grasp what it means. Occasionally a question allows for a variety of answers and is meant to help you explore the passage from several angles. "Grow!" questions are intended to elicit a personal response by helping you examine your life in light of the values and truths that you uncover through your study of the Scripture passage and its setting. Under the headings "Reflect!" and "Act!" we offer suggestions to help you respond concretely to the challenges posed by the passage.

Finally, pertinent quotations from the Fathers of the Church as well as insights from contemporary writers appear throughout each session. Coupled with relevant selections from the *Catechism of the Catholic Church* and information about the history, geography, and culture of first-century Palestine, these selections (called "In the Spotlight") add new layers of understanding and insight to your study.

As is true with any other learning resource, you will benefit the most from this study by writing your answers to the questions in the spaces provided. The simple act of writing can help you formulate your thoughts more clearly—and will also give you a record of your reflections and spiritual growth that you can return to in the future to see how much God has accomplished in your life. End your reading or study with a prayer thanking God for what you have learned—and ask the Holy Spirit to guide you in living out the call you have been given as a Christian in the world today.

Although the Scripture passages to be studied and the related verses for your reflection are printed in full in each guide (from the New Revised Standard Version Bible: Catholic Edition), you will find it helpful to have a Bible on hand for looking up other passages and cross-references or for comparing different translations.

The format of the guides in The Word Among Us Keys to the Bible series is especially well suited for use in small groups. Some recommendations and practical tips for using this guide in a Bible discussion group are offered on pages 100–103.

As you use this book to unlock the meaning of Jesus' miracles and grow in your faith, may the Holy Spirit draw you closer to Jesus, increase your love for him, and widen your vision of his kingdom.

The Word Among Us Press

Introduction
Understanding the Miracles of Jesus

God created us out of love. He wanted to share his very life with us. The fellowship and communion that he desired was broken, however, when Adam and Eve sinned in the garden of Eden. Because of their disobedience, humanity was separated from God and became subject to sickness, suffering, and death. Yet in his great mercy, God promised to reverse the consequences of this first sin. He fulfilled that promise in Jesus Christ, the Word made flesh.

Entrusted with his Father's mission to redeem mankind, Jesus began his public ministry, "teaching in their synagogues and proclaiming the good news of the kingdom and curing every disease and every sickness among the people" (Matthew 4:23). Indeed, after being anointed by the Spirit at his baptism, he identified himself as the one of whom the prophet Isaiah had spoken:

"The Spirit of the Lord is upon me,
   because he has anointed me
      to bring good news to the poor.
He has sent me to proclaim release to the captives
   and recovery of sight to the blind,
      to let the oppressed go free,
to proclaim the year of the Lord's favor."
                    —Luke 4:18-19 (see also Isaiah 61:1-2)

"Today this scripture has been fulfilled in your hearing" (Luke 4:21), Jesus declared to his fellow townspeople in the synagogue at Nazareth. As the *Catechism of the Catholic Church* notes, Jesus accompanied his teaching "with 'mighty works and wonders and signs' [Acts 2:22], which manifest that the kingdom is present in him and attest that he was the promised Messiah" (547).

Power Came Out from Him

The Greek word for "power," *dunamis,* is also the root of the word "dynamic." Divine power and dynamism radiated from Jesus and drew people to him: "All in the crowd were trying to touch him, for power came out from him and healed all of them" (Luke 6:19). In confronting sickness, sin, Satan, and even death, Jesus acted with the power and sovereign authority that were his as the Son of God, the Messiah-Redeemer.

Jesus' miracles did more than manifest his mighty power, though. They also communicated the love and compassion of God for his people. Jesus performed healings on the Sabbath—among them, restoring a man's withered hand and straightening the bent back of a woman—even though he knew he would be criticized by the Pharisees for doing so. He sometimes cured people of their physical ailments while at the same time healing them spiritually by forgiving their sins. The gospels often tell of Jesus' compassion when he performed a miracle, such as the time when he restored the life of the widow's only son in Nain (Luke 7:11-23).

Although there's no doubt that Jesus' miracles made a sensation, he didn't perform miracles to call attention to himself or enhance his reputation. In fact, he refused to do extraordinary deeds for his own advantage or glorification, rejecting Satan's urgings to turn stones into bread and to display his power by throwing himself from the pinnacle of the temple. He also refused to satisfy the Sadducees' and Pharisees' demand to "show them a sign from heaven" (Matthew 16:1-4) and Herod's desire to "see him perform some sign" (Luke 23:8). Rather, the miracles Jesus worked demonstrated his divine mission of redemption and expressed the saving power and mercy of God.

Accounts of Jesus' miracles make up a significant portion of the text of the gospels and record the variety of ways he revealed his divine power. Some restored people to wholeness and well-being through physical healing, the forgiveness of sins, or deliverance from evil spirits. Several revealed Jesus' authority over natural elements, such as when he multiplied the loaves and fish, transformed water into wine at Cana, and calmed a violent storm. Still other miraculous events—for instance, Jesus' transfiguration and his walk on the waters of the Sea of Galilee—were "epiphanies" of Jesus' glory.

These extraordinary deeds were not merely physical marvels that overturned the laws of nature. Rather, they were divine acts that *transcended* the natural order of the physical world—reminders that the kingdom of God transcends that physical world, as well. Theologically speaking, Jesus' miracles were "above nature"—signs that, in the spiritual order, had moral and religious character and revealed the nature and goodness of God.

Although the scribes and Pharisees didn't deny Jesus' ability to perform miraculous healings, they challenged the authority with which he performed them. Despite the evidence, some people rejected Jesus; others even accused him of acting by the power of Satan. One of the reasons the chief priests and Pharisees sought to kill Jesus was that they felt threatened by his power to work miracles and by his growing popularity with the crowds who witnessed them.

Historical Realities

The public character of Jesus' miracles is clearly recorded. From a historical perspective, it is indisputable that Jesus was recognized as a healer. His deeds were known by the crowds and generated great excitement among those who witnessed them. Indeed, it was because of his miraculous works that many regarded him as a great prophet. There is no evidence that Jesus' contemporaries denied the fact that he worked miracles, even though they disputed that God was the source of his ability to perform them. The miraculous nature of Jesus' deeds was confirmed by many eyewitnesses who later passed on accounts of them to the early Christian communities.

Jesus' miracles are not to be dismissed simply as ordinary events given grander meanings through the eyes of faith. They are actual physical realities that cannot be explained by natural or earthly causes. Nor are they mere symbols—although they do indeed contain symbolic resonances and a depth of symbolic meaning. The gospels not only record the memory of the actual events but often reveal the many levels of meaning found in them. For example, the healing of the blind man recounted in John 9 illustrates not only the restoration of the man's physical sight but also the removal of spiritual blindness and the attainment of spiritual insight and enlightenment. Similarly, Jesus' calming of the tempestuous wind and waves with a word of command points to the care and protection he still exercises over the church when it faces "storms." Feeding the hungry crowds by multiplying the loaves is a sign that Jesus himself is the Bread of Life and also alludes to the messianic banquet at the end of time. That these miraculous events have symbolic, theological, and ecclesial meanings contained in them does not discredit or reduce the authenticity of the miracles themselves.

Occasionally the accounts of Jesus' miracles vary in their details and their chronological placement in the gospels. Such variations reflect the processes by which the gospel tradition took shape and the way in which the gospels were written. First, Jesus worked his miracles. Then witnesses of these miracles recounted what they had seen as a way of spreading the good news of the salvation Jesus had brought. These oral stories were repeated and handed down over the years, and some were recorded in writings that predate the gospels. Finally, under the inspiration of the Holy Spirit, Matthew, Mark, Luke, and John drew upon all the material they found in the church's living tradition and wrote their gospels. When the original chronology of Jesus' actions or particular miracles was uncertain to them, they inserted them into the literary structure of their gospels with careful consideration of where these miracles would appropriately illustrate Jesus' mission and underscore his teachings.

The Evangelists did not invent or embellish the stories of Jesus' miracles, but they did present them from their individual perspectives and points of view. Mark's gospel closely associates Jesus' miracles with the proclamation of the good news of the kingdom, and through them reveals the person of Jesus, his power, his mission of redemption, and the establishment of God's reign. The Gospel of Matthew offers the outlook of an instructor or catechist, with its author highlighting people's professions of faith in Jesus, ways in which Jesus fulfilled Old Testament prophecies, and the significance of his teachings and miracles to the developing church. The gospel written by the physician-Evangelist Luke portrays Jesus as the prophet-Messiah sent by God to bring salvation and deliverance. Luke records Jesus' miracles—frequently with some medical detail—in the framework of Jesus' teachings, in order to illustrate how the kingdom of God was made present. John chose to recount only seven of Jesus' miracles, and he presented them as "signs" and "works" that manifested Christ's glory and bore witness that he had been sent by God.

Good News Made Visible

Jesus' miracles are, in fact, rich in their "sign value." Noted theologian and Scripture scholar René Latourelle has called them "the good news itself made visible."[1] We recognize in them signs of the power of God, signs of the coming of the Messiah and of the kingdom of God, signs of the compassion and love of God, signs of Christ's glory, and signs of the age to come.

Jesus himself pointed to the messianic signs foretold by Isaiah, which were fulfilled in him. When the disciples of John the Baptist asked, "Are you the one who is to come, or are we to wait for another?" Jesus said, "Go and tell John what you hear and see: the blind receive their sight, the lame walk, the lepers are cleansed, the deaf hear, the dead are raised, and the poor have good news brought to them" (Matthew 11:2-5; see also Isaiah 35:5-6).

When the apostle Peter addressed the Israelites on Pentecost, he told them of Jesus of Nazareth and the "deeds of power, wonders, and signs that God did through him among you" (Acts 2:22). Later, he spoke to the gentile Cornelius and his household of "how God anointed Jesus of Nazareth with the Holy Spirit and with power; how he went about doing good and healing all who were oppressed by the devil, for God was with him" (10:38). As the *Catechism of the Catholic Church* explains, "The signs worked by Jesus attest that the Father has sent him. They invite belief in him. To those who turn to him in faith, he grants what they ask. So miracles strengthen faith in the One who does his Father's works; they bear witness that he is the Son of God" (548).

The miracles that Jesus performed announced that the kingdom of God was breaking forth in the world. By his marvelous acts of healing and forgiveness, Jesus showed God's mercy toward those who were without hope—the weak, the ill, the sinful. The Son of God used his divine power in the service of love, moved with pity toward those in distress. Thus, "Christ's compassion toward the sick and his many healings of every kind of infirmity are a resplendent sign that 'God has visited his people' and that the Kingdom of God is close at hand" (*Catechism of the Catholic Church*, 1503).

The Greek word *simeion*—"sign"—is used seventeen times in the Gospel of John and sixty times throughout the rest of the New Testament. Chapters 1–12 of John's gospel have been called the Book of Signs because of the sign-miracles described there. For John, the mighty deeds that Jesus performed were signs that "revealed his glory" (John 2:11) and revealed the power of God working through him.

Finally, while the miracles occurred in the physical world of Jesus' day, they also prefigure greater realities to come, when "a new heaven and earth" (Isaiah 65:17; 2 Peter 3:13; Revelation 21:1) will be revealed. Restoring health to the ill and life to those who have died hints at the transformation that will take place at the end of time, when "this perishable body puts on imperishability, and this mortal body puts on immortality" (1 Corinthians 15:53).

Jesus' Invitation to Us

When Jesus worked miracles two thousand years ago, he manifested his love and compassion and called men and women to faith in him and his mission. These miraculous events still have something to say to us: they are Jesus' invitation to open ourselves to receive his mercy and to embrace the salvation he came to proclaim to us.

Today God continues to work miracles in our midst to bring us to wholeness and deeper conversion to him. Just as the father who sought freedom and deliverance for his child cried, "Lord, I believe; help my unbelief!" (Mark 9:24), so can we ask God to increase our faith. And just as the woman with the hemorrhage reached out to Jesus, saying and knowing in her heart, "If I only touch his cloak, I will be made well" (Matthew 9:21), so can we reach out to him now. Jesus is eager to answer us with miraculous signs of his presence and love and healing power.

Jeanne Kun

[1] For readers who are interested in a faith-filled, detailed, and scholarly examination of Jesus' miracles and their significance, I recommend René Latourelle's work *The Miracles of Jesus and the Theology of Miracles* (Mahwah, NJ: Paulist Press, 1988).

Wine in Abundance

John 2:1-12

¹ On the third day there was a wedding in Cana of Galilee, and the mother of Jesus was there. ²Jesus and his disciples had also been invited to the wedding. ³When the wine gave out, the mother of Jesus said to him, "They have no wine." ⁴And Jesus said to her, "Woman, what concern is that to you and to me? My hour has not yet come." ⁵His mother said to the servants, "Do whatever he tells you." ⁶Now standing there were six stone water jars for the Jewish rites of purification, each holding twenty or thirty gallons. ⁷Jesus said to them, "Fill the jars with water." And they filled them up to the brim. ⁸He said to them, "Now draw some out, and take it to the chief steward." So they took it. ⁹When the steward tasted the water that had become wine, and did not know where it came from (though the servants who had drawn the water knew), the steward called the bridegroom ¹⁰and said to him, "Everyone serves the good wine first, and then the inferior wine after the guests have become drunk. But you have kept the good wine until now." ¹¹Jesus did this, the first of his signs, in Cana of Galilee, and revealed his glory; and his disciples believed in him.

¹² After this he went down to Capernaum with his mother, his brothers, and his disciples; and they remained there a few days.

> This first miracle, in appearance the least "spiritual" of all, prepared them for what was to come, [and] introduced them to the unimaginable mystery.
> —François Mauriac, *Life of Jesus*

At the wedding feast in Cana we catch a glimpse of Jesus' kindness, the warmth of his personality, and his enjoyment of a good party. "I cannot imagine Jesus sitting alone with a serious face," wrote Jean Vanier, founder of L'Arche, in *Drawn into the Mystery of Jesus through the Gospel of John*. "Instead, I see him a part of the celebration, singing with everybody else, rejoicing in the festivity, profoundly happy to celebrate with people he knows and loves. . . . Jesus is so beautifully human!" Yet at this feast much more than Jesus' humanity and empathy was made evident—the divine glory of Jesus was manifested at Cana.

Cana isn't far from Jesus' hometown of Nazareth, so it's likely that the wedding Jesus and Mary attended was that of close relatives or neighbors. To run out of wine would have been quite an embarrassment for the newlyweds, since Middle Eastern hospitality demanded that hosts care for their guests graciously. So, at his mother's discreet request—the only record in Scripture of Mary's asking her son to fill a need—Jesus remedied the awkward situation.

Mary simply told Jesus, "They have no wine" (John 2:3)—and initially he replied that his "hour" had not yet come (2:4). Mary's words, however, implied more than the expectation that her son would do a favor for the bride and groom. She was prompting him to do something out of the ordinary (for surely she didn't merely think that Jesus would send his disciples to buy more wine). And, in this way, Mary was releasing Jesus from his responsibilities at home and suggesting that he now take up his divine work. Ultimately, when Jesus acted at his mother's urging and began to reveal himself by his action at Cana, he signaled that the fulfillment of his hour—that is, his redemptive mission, his passion and death, his resurrection and ascension in glory (7:30; 8:20; 12:27; 16:32; 17:1)—was drawing near.

"Fill the jars with water. . . . Now draw some out, and take it to the chief steward" (John 2:7-8). With these simple instructions to the waiters, Jesus changed 120 gallons of ordinary water into fine wine. This miraculous transformation was effected by his creative power and divine authority. The abundant quantity of wine highlights the greatness of the miracle as well as the generosity of God.

An abundance of wine is one of the dominant images that characterized the visions of the messianic era foretold by the ancient prophets of Israel (Isaiah 25:6; Joel 3:18; Amos 9:13-14). And the wedding feast mirrors the Old Testament image of marriage as an expression of God's relationship to Israel (Isaiah 54:5-6; 62:4-5; Hosea 2:19-20). In the New Testament, this messianic age is likened to a wedding banquet (Matthew 22:1-14; Revelation 19:9). When Jesus changed the water held in jars used for Jewish ritual purification (John 2:6) into wine, he was hinting that the messianic age had now arrived. With this "new wine" (Luke 5:33-39), a new era had begun—an era in which Jesus himself is the bridegroom (John 3:29). For, by providing wine in plenty at a marriage feast—a responsibility of the bridegroom—he pointed to his identity as divine bridegroom and Messiah and to the new covenant he was to accomplish by his life and death.

John called this miracle of Jesus a "sign" (John 2:11)—the first among many that the Evangelist recorded in his gospel. The mighty work that Jesus did in Cana was not simply an extraordinary act done out of kindness and compassion. It was a sign that revealed Jesus' glory and unveiled God's power and love actively working through him—and a sign that invited all who witnessed it to faith in the one whom God sent to fulfill his plan of salvation.

Understand!

1. John wrote that the wedding in Cana occurred "on the third day" (John 2:1), that is, three days after Jesus' encounter with Nathanael (1:43-51). What significance do you see in this chronology? What other events in Scripture involve a time framework of three days?

_____

_____

_____

_____

_____

_____

2. Why, in your opinion, did Jesus perform this miracle? Note the reasons that are stated in the text as well as those that seem to be hinted at or implied. What impact do you think this miracle had on the various people who witnessed it?

_____

_____

_____

_____

_____

3. What do Mary's presence, words, and actions at the wedding at Cana and afterward at Capernaum indicate to you about her? About her relationship with her son?

_____

_____

_____

_____

_____

_____

_____

4. Is faith evident in this scene? If so, in what ways? Whose faith? What do the results of the servants' actions suggest about the importance of obedience?

_____

_____

_____

_____

_____

_____

_____

_____

5. How is the miracle at Cana a sign of the coming kingdom of God? What is its value as a sign? (Note that six other "signs" are recounted in the Gospel of John: the healing of the official's son—4:46-54; the healing of the paralyzed man—5:2-9; the multiplication of the loaves—6:1-14; the healing of the blind man—9:1-41; and the raising of Lazarus—11:1-44.)

_____

_____

_____

_____

_____

_____

_____

The sign of water turned into wine at Cana already announces the Hour of Jesus' glorification. It makes manifest the fulfillment of the wedding feast in the Father's kingdom, where the faithful will drink the new wine that has become the Blood of Christ. (1335)

The Church attaches great importance to Jesus' presence at the wedding at Cana. She sees in it the confirmation of the goodness of marriage and the proclamation that thenceforth marriage will be an efficacious sign of Christ's presence. (1613)

The Gospel reveals to us how Mary prays and intercedes in faith. At Cana, the mother of Jesus asks her son for the needs of a wedding feast; this is the sign of another feast—that of the wedding of the Lamb where he gives his body and blood at the request of the Church, his Bride. (2618)

Grow!

1. Mary brought the newlyweds' need to Jesus' attention. When have you been an advocate for someone in need? How were you able to help? What could you do to make intercession a more active and effective part of your prayer life?

_____

_____

_____

_____

_____

2. "Do whatever he tells you" (John 2:5) are the last words of Mary recorded in Scripture. Think of a time when you did something because you felt that Jesus told you to do it. Was it easy or difficult for you to obey him? What were the results?

_____

_____

_____

_____

_____

_____

3. The miracle at Cana shows Jesus' kindness and concern for the bride and groom. Recall a situation when someone cared for your needs. How did their attention affect you? How did they reflect the face of Christ to you?

_____

_____

_____

_____

_____

_____

4. Jesus changed ordinary water into wine—in a plentiful quantity—at Cana. Write a prayer asking Jesus either to transform some "ordinary water" in your life into "good wine" (John 2:10) or to provide abundantly in an area of your life where you feel a lack or limitation.

_____

_____

_____

_____

_____

_____

5. The disciples "believed in him" after they had seen Jesus transform water into wine (John 2:11). What "signs" of God at work in your life have caused your faith to grow and deepen?

_____

_____

_____

_____

_____

_____

_____

▶ In the Spotlight
Jewish Wedding Customs

In Jesus' day, it was customary in Palestine for the bridegroom and his friends to carry the bride in a chair from her parents' house to the groom's house in a torchlit procession. There the couple—who had already been pledged to one another at their betrothal—concluded the marriage ceremony.

Nuptial festivities followed, which lasted from three to eight days and included singing, dancing, and feasting (Genesis 29:27; Judges 14:10, 12, 17).

Relatives and friends—even townspeople and people passing through—came to greet the bride and groom and join in their joy. Flowing wine added to the celebratory atmosphere and cheered the hearts of the guests. In fact, the Aramaic word used to describe a wedding feast is *mistita*, which has the same root as the word "drink" and literally means "drink-festival."

Hospitality was highly esteemed in the culture of the Middle East, so to fail in one's duties as a gracious and generous host leaves a blot on the family's reputation. In first-century Palestine, a bridegroom and his family could even have been heavily fined or taken to court for not providing sufficiently for their guests. Thus, by miraculously providing wine in abundance when it had run out at the wedding in Cana, Jesus saved the newlyweds from social embarrassment and from the displeasure of their guests and prevented a disruption of the festivities.

Reflect!

1. Think about how you and your family or friends celebrate special occasions such as weddings, birthdays, graduations, first Communions, and anniversaries. What could you do to make your celebrations more meaningful and more festive for your guests?

2. Reflect on the following Scripture passages to enhance your understanding of Jesus' mission as the Messiah:

> How beautiful upon the mountains
>   are the feet of the messenger
>   who announces peace,
> who brings good news,
>   who announces salvation,
>   who says to Zion, "Your God reigns."
>   —Isaiah 52:7

> Then Jesus went about all the cities and villages, teaching in their synagogues, and proclaiming the good news of the kingdom, and curing every disease and every sickness. When he saw the crowds, he had compassion for them, because they were harassed and helpless, like sheep without a shepherd.
>
> —Matthew 9:35-36

[T]hey brought to [Jesus] all who were sick or possessed with demons. And the whole city was gathered around the door. And he cured many who were sick with various diseases, and cast out many demons; and he would not permit the demons to speak, because they knew him.

In the morning, while it was still very dark, he got up and went out to a deserted place, and there he prayed. And Simon and his companions hunted for him. When they found him, they said to him, "Everyone is searching for you." He answered, "Let us go on to the neighboring towns, so that I may proclaim the message there also; for that is what I came out to do." And he went throughout Galilee, proclaiming the message in their synagogues and casting out demons.

—Mark 1:32-39

When [Jesus] came to Nazareth, where he had been brought up, he went to the synagogue on the sabbath day, as was his custom. He stood up to read, and the scroll of the prophet Isaiah was given to him. He unrolled the scroll and found the place where it was written:

"The Spirit of the Lord is upon me,
　　because he has anointed me to bring good news
　　　　to the poor.
He has sent me to proclaim release to the captives
　　and recovery of sight to the blind,
　　　　to let the oppressed go free,
to proclaim the year of the Lord's favor."

—Luke 4:16-19 (see also Isaiah 61:1-2)

▶ In the Spotlight
Mary Intercedes for Us

When the wine gave out at Cana, it is interesting to note that Mary was more concerned with the guests than was the wine-steward, for it was she, and not he, who noticed their need of wine. Mary turned to her Divine Son in a perfect spirit of prayer. Completely confident in Him and trusting in His mercy, she said: "They have no wine left" (John 2:3).

It was not a personal request; she was already a mediatrix for all who were seeking the fulness of joy. She has never been just a spectator, but a full participant willingly involving herself in the needs of others. The mother used the special power which she had as a mother over her Son, a power generated by mutual love.

—Archbishop Fulton J. Sheen, *Life of Christ*

To understand Mary's great goodness, let us remember what the Gospel says. . . . There was a shortage of wine, which naturally worried the married couple. No one asks the Blessed Virgin to intervene and request her Son to come to the rescue of the couple. But Mary's heart cannot but take pity on the unfortunate couple; . . . it stirs her to act as intercessor and ask her Son for the miracle, even though no one asks her to. . . . If our Lady acted like this without being asked, what would she not have done if they actually asked her to intervene?

—St. Alphonsus Liguori, *Sunday Sermons*

Mary can teach us kindness. . . . "They have no wine," she told Jesus at Cana. Let us, like her, be aware of the needs of the poor, be they spiritual or material, and let us, like her, give generously of the love and grace we are granted.

—Blessed Mother Teresa of Calcutta, *Love: A Fruit Always in Season*

Act!

"God is able to provide you with every blessing in abundance, so that by always having enough of everything, you may share abundantly in every good work." (2 Corinthians 9:8)

This week, reach out to someone in a way that will communicate to him or her God's personal love and care, as well as his abundant generosity.

▶ In the Spotlight
God's Abundant Provision

Marguerite d'Youville founded the Sisters of Charity of Montreal, commonly known as the Grey Nuns, after she was widowed. During the eighteenth-century colonization of French Canada and the hardships of the French and Indian War (1754–1763), she and her sisters ran a hospital for the sick and infirm as well as an orphanage for abandoned babies. Blessed John XXIII called her the Mother of Universal Charity. St. Marguerite d'Youville was canonized by Pope John Paul II in 1990.

Once, after checking her accounts, Mother d'Youville discovered that she had only one small silver coin left. At that moment, a poor woman came to claim her payment for nursing a baby in their care—a payment of the exact amount of the coin. Marguerite reached into her pocket, only to find a whole handful of coins! Amazed, she reached into her other pocket and brought out yet another handful! At another time, when the sisters and their patients were close to starving, six barrels of flour inexplicably "appeared" in their dining room. The Eternal Father never failed to care for his daughters and for the poor they served.

—*In the Land I Have Shown You: The Stories of 16 Saints and Christian Heroes of North America*

Health for the Body and Soul

Luke 5:17-26

17 One day, while [Jesus] was teaching, Pharisees and teachers of the law were sitting near by (they had come from every village of Galilee and Judea and from Jerusalem); and the power of the Lord was with him to heal. 18Just then some men came, carrying a paralyzed man on a bed. They were trying to bring him in and lay him before Jesus; 19but finding no way to bring him in because of the crowd, they went up on the roof and let him down with his bed through the tiles into the middle of the crowd in front of Jesus. 20When he saw their faith, he said, "Friend, your sins are forgiven you." 21Then the scribes and the Pharisees began to question, "Who is this who is speaking blasphemies? Who can forgive sins but God alone?" 22When Jesus perceived their questionings, he answered them, "Why do you raise such questions in your hearts? 23Which is easier, to say, 'Your sins are forgiven you,' or to say, 'Stand up and walk'? 24But so that you may know that the Son of Man has authority on earth to forgive sins"—he said to the one who was paralyzed—"I say to you, stand up and take your bed and go to your home." 25Immediately he stood up before them, took what he had been lying on, and went to his home, glorifying God. 26Amazement seized all of them, and they glorified God and were filled with awe, saying, "We have seen strange things today."

(See also Matthew 9:1-8 and Mark 2:1-12)

> Moved by the faith of those who lower the paralytic into his presence, Jesus speaks the word of forgiveness, thus announcing the breaking-in of the kingdom into the twisted frame of the paralytic's existence, and assuring him of God's acceptance.
> —Herman Hendrickx, CICM, *The Miracle Stories of the Synoptic Gospels*

Many people directly encountered Jesus in this scene that took place early in his Galilean ministry—scribes, Pharisees, those who had gathered to listen to Jesus teach, the friends of the paralyzed man, and the afflicted man himself. Jesus' surprising words and actions evoked a strong response in each of these people, yet how greatly those responses varied!

Was it the paralyzed man's own faith and hopes that spurred his friends to help him seek healing? Or was the man so wholly incapacitated and disheartened that his friends simply acted on their own initiative? In either case, paralysis prevented the man from coming to Jesus on his own. So his friends—fired with their faith in Jesus' power and willingness to heal—went to great lengths on his behalf, boldly determined to overcome any obstacle. Thus, one unable to help himself was helped by the active faith and intercession of others.

When Jesus saw the man's condition, he said, "Your sins are forgiven you" (Luke 5:20). Just imagine how surprising those words must have sounded to those present, for hadn't the man come to ask for physical healing? But Jesus was not simply concerned with his palsied limbs; he cared first and foremost about the man's spiritual well-being. In ancient Jewish society, many considered sickness to be a punishment for sin. Although Jesus didn't sanction this outlook, he did recognize that from the perspective of eternity, spiritual wellness was far more essential than physical wellness. Through the forgiveness of sins, he assured the man of God's love and restored him to spiritual health. The reign of God that Jesus had come to proclaim was now clearly at hand (Mark 1:15).

The criticism of the scribes and Pharisees contrasted sharply with the admiration of the crowd who had eagerly gathered around the house to hear this extraordinary teacher. These experts of the law complained when Jesus exercised the divine prerogative to forgive sin (Psalm 103:3, 12; Isaiah 43:25). They challenged Jesus' authority and accused him of blasphemy—an offense punishable by stoning (Leviticus 24:16)—because they failed to recognize his true identity (Luke 5:24). This was a pivotal encounter, for it marked the beginning of the Pharisees' hostility toward Jesus.

Jesus' response to the Pharisees' questionings was an adroit one. He asked whether it was easier to tell the man that his sins were forgiven or to tell him to get up and walk. By performing the seemingly more difficult task—that of visibly curing the man's paralysis—he likely convinced many present that he was also capable of performing the intangible, imperceptible act of forgiving his sins. In other words, Jesus visibly healed the man's body to confirm the invisible restoration of his soul. In this way he showed that he had the power to cure the malignant effects on the whole human person of both sickness and sin. By doing what only God can do—forgive sin and instantly cure illness—Jesus showed his divinity and his power to defeat evil.

At Jesus' command—"stand up"—the formerly paralyzed man rose, picked up his bed, and returned home to enjoy the new life and freedom he had received, praising God as he went (Luke 5:24-25). The bystanders were astonished at what they had seen and also glorified God (5:26)—reactions that would often be repeated by the crowds who eagerly followed Jesus and witnessed his mighty works (7:16; 13:13; 17:15; 18:43; 23:47). The Pharisees too might have been amazed at Jesus' power, for they had seen with their own eyes the miraculous healing he had performed. However, they were often inclined to attribute his healing power to the devil rather than to God (see Matthew 12:24)—especially since he frequently violated their law by healing on the Sabbath. Hence, they couldn't accept his ability to forgive sin, because they couldn't accept his divinity. Not long after this, they began to plot to destroy him (Mark 3:6).

Understand!

1. What important information did Luke provide in verse 17 to set the scene for his account of Jesus' miracle? How does this contribute to your understanding of the event?

_____

_____

_____

_____

_____

_____

_____

2. Why did Jesus forgive the paralyzed man's sins before he healed his physical disability? What have you learned about Jesus from the way he related to this man?

_____

_____

_____

_____

_____

_____

_____

3. What relationship, if any, do you see in this scene between faith and physical healing? Between faith and forgiveness of sin?

_____

_____

_____

_____

_____

_____

4. Jesus "perceived the questionings" (Luke 5:22) and secret thoughts of the scribes and Pharisees and "knew what is in everyone" (John 2:25; see also Matthew 9:4; 12:25; Luke 6:8; 11:17). How did this knowledge affect Jesus? What impact did it have on his interactions with others?

_____

_____

_____

_____

_____

_____

_____

5. What was Jesus' response to the accusations of the scribes and Pharisees? What does this response reveal about his understanding of human nature?

_____

_____

_____

_____

_____

_____

▶ In the Spotlight
Wisdom from the Church Fathers

When the Savior says to him, "Man, your sins are forgiven you," he addresses this to humankind in general. For those who believe in him, being healed of the diseases of the soul, will receive forgiveness of sins which they formerly committed. He may also mean this: "I must heal your soul before I heal your body. If this is not done, by obtaining strength to walk, you will only sin more. Even though you have not asked

for this, I as God see the maladies of the soul which brought on you this disease."
—St. Cyril of Alexandria, *Commentary on Luke*

Brethren, if we but chose to look into every paralysis of our mind, and see our soul as it lies abandoned upon its bed of sin, we should see it clearly as Christ sees us, urging us, even unwilling, towards his saving remedies.
—St. Peter Chrysologos

Grow!

1. Do you ever feel that Jesus is "inaccessible" to you or "unreachable"? If so, what "crowds" or blocks your access to him? What could you do to remove such impediments?

_____

_____

_____

_____

_____

_____

2. Why do you think it is sometimes difficult for us to believe that Jesus loves us in spite of our sins and weaknesses? Have you ever been so "paralyzed" that you couldn't ask Jesus for healing or forgiveness? If so, what helped you to get past the paralysis and seek his mercy?

_____

_____

_____

_____

_____

_____

3. The paralyzed man's friends were undeterred in their determination to reach Jesus. Recall a time when you made a real effort to bring someone to Christ. Were there any obstacles that had to be overcome to help him or her draw near to the Lord? What happened as a result of your efforts?

_____

_____

_____

_____

_____

_____

4. Who might be in need of the support of your faith or intercession right now? In what concrete way could you share your faith or encourage him or her?

_____

_____

_____

_____

_____

5. Think of a time when you received Christ's forgiveness for your sins or forgiveness from a person whom you had offended. In what way did this forgiveness set you free or restore you to spiritual health?

_____

_____

_____

_____

_____

The Lord Jesus Christ, physician of our souls and bodies, who forgave the sins of the paralytic and restored him to bodily health, has willed that his Church continue, in the power of the Holy Spirit, his work of healing and salvation, even among her own members. This is the purpose of the two sacraments of healing: the sacrament of Penance and the sacrament of Anointing of the Sick. (1421)

Only God forgives sins. Since he is the Son of God, Jesus says of himself, "The Son of man has authority on earth to forgive sins" and exercises this divine power: "Your sins are forgiven." Further, by virtue of his divine authority he gives this power to men to exercise in his name. (1441)

[Christ] personally addresses every sinner: "My son, your sins are forgiven." He is the physician tending each one of the sick who need him to cure them. He raises them up and reintegrates them into fraternal communion. Personal confession is thus the form most expressive of reconciliation with God and with the Church. (1484)

Reflect!

1. Identify various forms of "paralysis" that affect you, such as fear of what others think of you, complacency, or anxiety. How do these conditions hinder your ability to respond to God? In prayer, ask the Lord to free you from your paralysis.

2. Reflect on the following Scripture passages to deepen your understanding of God's mercy and forgiveness:

> Thus says the LORD, . . .
> I, I am He
>   who blots out your transgressions
>   for my own sake,
>   and I will not remember your sins.
> —Isaiah 43:14, 25

> [A]s he sat at dinner in Levi's house, many tax collectors and sinners were also sitting with Jesus and his disciples—for there were many who followed him. When the scribes of the Pharisees saw that he was eating with sinners and tax collectors, they said to his disciples, "Why does he eat with tax collectors and sinners?" When Jesus heard this, he said to them, "Those who are well have no need of a physician, but those who are sick; I have come to call not the righteous but sinners."
> —Mark 2:15-17

> Jesus was left alone with the woman [caught in adultery] standing before him. Jesus straightened up and said to her, "Woman, where are they? Has no one condemned you?" She said, "No one, sir." And Jesus said, "Neither do I condemn you. Go your way, and from now on do not sin again."
> —John 8:9-11

> [T]he disciples rejoiced when they saw the Lord. Jesus said to them again, "Peace be with you. As the Father has sent me, so I send you." When he had said this, he breathed on them and said to them, "Receive the Holy

Spirit. If you forgive the sins of any, they are forgiven them; if you retain the sins of any, they are retained."

—John 20:20-23

Are any among you sick? They should call for the elders of the church and have them pray over them, anointing them with oil in the name of the Lord. The prayer of faith will save the sick, and the Lord will raise them up; and anyone who has committed sins will be forgiven. Therefore, confess your sins to one another, and pray for one another, so that you may be healed.

—James 5:14-16

▶ In the Spotlight
"Even When No One Will Forgive, God Does"

I am incarcerated for crimes that "decent people" find incomprehensible. I was a child molester. In the eyes of many, especially other inmates with violent crimes, I am viewed as the vilest of all, and this has caused me to believe myself "beyond redemption." I struggle to accept God's forgiveness. Flannery O'Connor, the Catholic novelist, wrote, "The central mystery of Christianity is that God would find humanity worth dying for." Only the truth of this statement keeps me going. Even when no one will forgive, God does. Even when I fail in my own efforts to love my worst enemies as much as I love God, Jesus still intercedes for me and cleanses me by his sacrifice.

—**Anonymous Prisoner,** *God Forgives, Can I?*

Act!

Jesus' words as he encountered the paralyzed man—"Friend, your sins are forgiven you"—are echoed in the Sacrament of Reconciliation, where pardon involves a personal encounter with Christ.

Go to confession this week. Ask the Holy Spirit to guide you in making a good examination of conscience in preparation for receiving the graces of the sacrament. Afterward, thank God for his gifts of forgiveness and reconciliation.

▶ In the Spotlight
Contemporary Voices

The fact that the man does not rise immediately upon the word of forgiveness shows that healing is more than forgiveness. But it also shows that forgiveness is the door to healing.
—**George Montague, SM,** *Mark: Good News for Hard Times*

When Jesus puts his hands on blind eyes, deaf ears, bent backs, paralyzed limbs, the Creator-God is at work through him, not merely patching up the rents in his old creation but really bringing in the new. It is true that the life he directly gives to broken bodies is natural life: the flesh that grows in leprous places will crumble one day and Lazarus will have to die again. But, the Bible never makes a sharp division between physical and spiritual healing, anymore than we can today with our awareness of our psychosomatic unity. When Christ heals, then and now, he heals the whole person, because the whole person stands open to God's re-creative power.
—**Maria Boulding,** *Prayer: Our Journey Home*

Lord of the Wind and Waves

Mark 4:35-41

35 On that day, when evening had come, [Jesus] said to [his disciples], "Let us go across to the other side." 36And leaving the crowd behind, they took him with them in the boat, just as he was. Other boats were with him. 37A great windstorm arose, and the waves beat into the boat, so that the boat was already being swamped. 38But he was in the stern, asleep on the cushion; and they woke him up and said to him, "Teacher, do you not care that we are perishing?" 39He woke up and rebuked the wind, and said to the sea, "Peace! Be still!" Then the wind ceased, and there was a dead calm. 40He said to them, "Why are you afraid? Have you still no faith?" 41And they were filled with great awe and said to one another, "Who then is this, that even the wind and the sea obey him?"

(See also Matthew 8:23-27 and Luke 8:22-25)

> The untroubled sleep of Jesus and his sovereign authority over wind and wave are a powerful invitation to recognize in him the one who can do all things.
> —René Latourelle, SJ, *The Miracles of Jesus and the Theology of Miracles*

At Jesus' initiative the apostles set out across the Sea of Galilee to the eastern shore, six or seven miles distant, as the sun was setting behind the Galilean hills (Mark 4:35). Tired after a long day of preaching and teaching, Jesus slept soundly in the stern of the boat, oblivious to the rising squall. This is the sole instance recorded in the gospels of Jesus sleeping, an image that vividly illustrates his humanness, as well as the hiddenness of his divine nature, which is a dominant theme in Mark's gospel.

Experienced fishermen that they were, Jesus' disciples were badly frightened by the violence of the storm. Following their master had gotten them into this life-threatening situation, and their anxious cry had a reproachful tone as they woke him: "Teacher, do you not care that we are perishing?" (Mark 4:38). *Melo,* the Greek verb used in this complaint, can also be translated "Does it not matter to you?" The same verb is found in Martha's question "Lord, do you not care that my sister has left me to do all the work by myself?" (Luke 10:40). In both instances, Jesus' response was the same: to calm the turbulence of troubled hearts and the storms that raged around him.

With a mere word of command—"Be still!" (Mark 4:39)—Jesus subdued the wind and the sea, showing his power over natural elements. Just as God brought the waters into being (Genesis 1:6-10), tamed roaring waves (Psalm 65:7), and parted the Red Sea before Moses and the Israelites (Exodus 14:21-22; Psalm 77:16, 19-20), Jesus exercised authority and showed mastery over the storm-tossed waters of the Sea of Galilee. "The waves are his creatures and behave as such by offering him the fealty of obedience," notes Scripture commentator Erasmo Leiva-Merikakis (*Fire of Mercy, Heart of the Word*).

In ancient times, the wind and sea were often seen as symbols of chaos. The way Jesus rebuked the elements may also imply that there was an evil force behind the storm, for he calmed the waves with the same command that he used to silence unclean spirits (Mark 1:25; Luke 4:35). It is noteworthy that this miraculous event occurred while Jesus was crossing the lake to pagan territory—the country of the Gerasenes—where he was extending his ministry to gentiles and was soon to confront the unclean spirit "Legion" and heal the man possessed by a demon (Mark 5:1-13). In each of the synoptic gospels, the report of the stilling the storm leads into a sequence recounting Jesus' authority and power in exorcising evil spirits, curing the ill, and raising the dead (Matthew 8:28–9:31; Mark 5:1-42; Luke 8:26-56). René Latourelle notes, "Jesus is victorious over death, sickness, sin, and the forces of nature, simply because in his very being he is God-among-us. It is not more difficult for him to control the wind and the sea than to prevail over sin and death" (*The Miracles of Jesus and the Theology of Miracles*).

When the terrified disciples woke Jesus, was it only to reproach him with a cry of desperation because they thought they were doomed? Even if their cry expressed an expectant faith that he could do something to save them, their understanding and faith were still deficient: for they did not yet realize that their teacher was the Son of God and that therefore they were safe all along. Finally, the disciples' fear of the storm turned into awe at Jesus' tremendous deed, and they wondered, "Who then is this, that even the wind and the sea obey him?" (Mark 4:41). Jesus' display of power awakened them to the mystery of his transcendence and identity.

The question of *who Jesus really is* is a recurring theme in the gospels (Luke 5:21; 7:49; 8:25). It is also a question each of us must answer in the depths of our own heart, especially when we are faced with the need of a Savior in the storms of life.

Understand!

1. Trace the changes in the disciples' emotions as the scene unfolds in Mark 4:35-41. What does the story indicate about their perceptions of Jesus and their relationship with him? About their faith or doubts and fears?

_____

_____

_____

_____

_____

_____

2. Many scholars believe that this story is based on Peter's memory of the incident. Identify details in Mark's description of the stilling of the storm that have the sound of eyewitness recollections. What purpose do these vivid details serve in the story? How do they contribute to its effect?

_____

_____

_____

_____

_____

_____

3. Read Matthew 8:23-27 and Luke 8:22-25. How do these other accounts of the calming of the storm complement Mark's? How do they expand your view and understanding of the apostles? Of Jesus?

_____

_____

_____

_____

_____

_____

_____

4. In your opinion, when Jesus' rebuked his apostles with the words "Why are you afraid? Have you still no faith?" (Mark 4:40), was he being too harsh or was he justified? Explain your answer. What do you think Jesus wanted his apostles to learn from his response to their fear?

_____

_____

_____

_____

_____

_____

_____

5. The early Christian community and the church fathers saw this story of a boat on the stormy sea as a metaphor for the church, the "barque (ship) of Peter." Read in this light, what lesson does this miracle story teach? What hope does it give to the people of God?

_____

_____

_____

_____

_____

_____

▶ In the Spotlight
Be Still!

In Mark's gospel, Jesus subdued the sea with a form of the Greek word *phimoo*, which we translate as "Be still!" (Mark 4:39). In its most literal translation, *phimoo* means "to close the mouth with a muzzle (*phimos*)."

Phimoo first appears in the Bible in Deuteronomy 25:4: "You shall not muzzle an ox while it is treading out the grain," implying that the animal deserves to be able to eat something for its efforts. Paul later used the same word in explaining that those who labor spiritually ought to be repaid materially by those who benefit from their labors: "For the scripture says, 'You shall not muzzle an ox while it is treading out the grain,' and 'The laborer deserves to be paid'" (1 Timothy 5:18; see also 1 Corinthians 9:9-11).

Phimoo is also used metaphorically to mean "to silence," "to render speechless," or "to subdue to stillness." Jesus used this same command, with which he stilled the raging sea, to free a man from an unclean spirit. He rebuked the spirit, "Be silent, and come out of him!" (Mark 1:25; Luke 4:35).

Grow!

1. Recall an occasion when you were "tossed about" by a severe "storm" in your life. How did you react? How did Jesus manifest his presence and power in that storm? How did your relationship with Jesus help you in that crisis?

_____

_____

_____

_____

_____

_____

_____

_____

2. Are any turbulent "waves"—for example, a financial crisis, a relationship difficulty, depression, family problems—threatening to overwhelm and capsize you right now? If so, visualize Jesus in the boat with you in the midst of the storm. Write a prayer expressing to him your need as well as your faith in his power and loving care for you.

_____

_____

_____

_____

_____

_____

_____

3. Do you sometimes feel that Jesus is "asleep in the boat," that is, unconcerned about you or unaware of your needs or the difficulties facing you? What is your prayer like then? What could you do to overcome such feelings?

_____

_____

_____

_____

_____

_____

_____

4. Jesus asked his disciples, "Why are you afraid? Have you still no faith?" (Mark 4:40). Has the Lord addressed similar words to you? If so, when? How has Jesus called you to trust him more? What could you do to increase your faith?

_____

_____

_____

_____

_____

_____

_____

5. Awed at Jesus' power, the disciples wondered who Jesus was. How would you answer this question, in light of what Jesus has done for you personally?

_____

_____

_____

_____

_____

_____

▶ In the Spotlight
Contemporary Voices

Following the example of the Apostles in the boat, Christians should seek Jesus' help, borrowing their words, "Save us, Lord; we are perishing." Then, when it seems we can bear it no longer, Jesus shows his power: "He rose and rebuked the winds and the sea; and there was a great calm."
—_The Navarre Bible: The Gospel of Saint Matthew_

The Savior is redeeming his disciples by making his profound serenity as God inhabit the same space as their frantic despair. . . . Jesus' sleeping presence represents the unobtrusive, but insistent, sustaining Presence of God at the center of his creation. When that center "awakens" and manifests itself in concrete action, it encompasses both man and the cosmos with nurturing goodness. Jesus awakens in order to chastise his disciples' lagging faith and thus awaken *them* to a higher life in the Spirit.

—Erasmo Leiva-Merikakis, *Fire of Mercy, Heart of the Word*

When the community or the individual goes through a storm and fears sinking, the disciple's faith is challenged to believe not only that Jesus is present and is caring for his own, but that he is also Lord of the chaos; his limitless power can meet and redeem the most terrifying disaster.

—George Montague, SM, *Mark: Good News for Hard Times*

Reflect!

1. Meditate on God's creative power as it is manifested in nature. What responses do the grandeur of nature and signs of God's power evoke in you? Awe? Worship? Fear? Gratitude? Have you ever seen God calm or overcome destructive forces in nature? If so, when? Have you ever wondered why God did not prevent destruction from happening? If so, why do you think he didn't intervene?

2. Reflect on the following Scripture passages that illustrate God's power over the forces of nature and the forces of evil:

> O Lord God of Hosts,
>> who is as mighty as you, O Lord?

Your faithfulness surrounds you.
You rule the raging of the sea;
   when its waves rise, you still them.
                   —Psalm 89:8-9

Some went down to the sea in ships,
   doing business on the mighty waters;
they saw the deeds of the LORD,
   his wondrous works in the deep.
For he commanded and raised the stormy wind,
   which lifted up the waves of the sea.
They mounted up to heaven,
    they went down to the depths;
   their courage melted away in their calamity;
they reeled and staggered like drunkards,
   and were at their wits' end.
Then they cried to the LORD in their trouble,
   and he brought them out from their distress;
he made the storm be still,
   and the waves of the sea were hushed.
Then they were glad because they had quiet,
   and he brought them to their desired haven.
Let them thank the LORD for his steadfast love,
   for his wonderful works to humankind.
Let them extol him in the congregation
    of the people,
   and praise him in the assembly of the elders.
                 —Psalm 107:23-32

They went to Capernaum; and when the sabbath came, he entered the synagogue and taught. They were astounded at his teaching, for he taught them as one having authority, and not as the scribes. Just then there was in their synagogue a man with an unclean spirit, and he cried out, "What have you to do with us, Jesus of Nazareth? Have you come to destroy us? I know who you are, the Holy One of God." But Jesus rebuked him, saying, "Be silent, and come out of him!" And the unclean spirit, convulsing him and crying with a loud voice, came out of him. They were all amazed, and they kept on asking one another, "What is this? A new teaching—with authority! He commands even the unclean spirits, and they obey him." At once his fame began to spread throughout the surrounding region of Galilee.

—Mark 1:21-28

Elijah was a human being like us, and he prayed fervently that it might not rain, and for three years and six months it did not rain on the earth. Then he prayed again, and the heaven gave rain and the earth yielded its harvest.

—James 5:17-18

▶ In the Spotlight
The Sea of Galilee

The Sea of Galilee is the world's lowest freshwater lake, situated seven hundred feet below sea level in a deep gash in the earth's surface known as the Great Rift Valley. It has a length of thirteen miles, a width up to eight miles, and a depth of as much as two hundred feet. The mountains of Lower Galilee rise to the west of the lake, and to the east, the volcanic hills of the Golan Heights. Its shores widen into fertile plains near Gennesaret and Bethsaida. The waters of the lake shimmer deep blue under Galilee's semitropical sun, fed by the Jordan River, which flows into the lake from the north and out at its southern tip.

The Sea of Galilee is called the Lake of Gennesaret in 1 Maccabees 11:67 and Luke 5:1. It is also known as the Sea of Tiberias (John 6:1; 21:1)—after the town on its southwest shore founded to honor the Roman emperor Tiberius—and as the Sea of Chinnereth, named for an important shore town in the Canaanite period (Numbers 34:11; Joshua 12:3).

The Sea of Galilee is normally calm in the summer months, but fierce squalls often arise quite abruptly in the winter and spring. Violent turbulence results without warning when the cool east wind *(sharkiyeh)* blows down the steep valleys cut into the mountains and clashes with the hot, humid air over the low-lying lake. Galilee's fishermen dread these sudden, severe storms.

Act!

This week, encourage and comfort someone you know who is facing a severe storm in life or whose faith is being battered by waves of doubt. Your loving concern for this person can reassure him or her of God's love and care and strengthen his or her faith.

▶ In the Spotlight
Wisdom from the Church Fathers

He who was sleeping was awakened and cast the sea into a sleep. He reveals the wakefulness of his divinity that never sleeps by the wakefulness of the sea that was now sleeping. He rebuked the wind and it became still. What is this power, or what is this goodness of Jesus? See, he subjected by force that which was not his. Our Lord showed that he was the Son of the Creator by means of the wind of the sea and by the spirits and demons that he silenced.

—St. Ephrem, *Commentary on Tatian's Diatessaron*

We are also sailing on a voyage, not from one land to another but from earth to heaven. Let us prepare our power of reasoning as a pilot able to conduct us on high, and let us gather a crew obedient to it. Let us prepare a strong ship, the kind that the buffeting and discouragements of this life will not submerge, or the wind of false pretense raise up, but will be sleek and swift. If we prepare the ship, pilot and the crew in this way, we will sail with a favoring wind and draw to ourselves the Son of God, the true Pilot. He will not permit our ship to be overwhelmed, even if countless winds blow. He will rebuke the winds and the sea and will bring about a great calm in place of the tempest.

—St. John Chrysostom, *Commentary on St. John I*

Restored to Life

Luke 7:11-23

¹¹ Soon afterwards [Jesus] went to a town called Nain, and his disciples and a large crowd went with him. ¹²As he approached the gate of the town, a man who had died was being carried out. He was his mother's only son, and she was a widow; and with her was a large crowd from the town. ¹³When the Lord saw her, he had compassion for her and said to her, "Do not weep." ¹⁴Then he came forward and touched the bier, and the bearers stood still. And he said, "Young man, I say to you, rise!" ¹⁵The dead man sat up and began to speak, and Jesus gave him to his mother. ¹⁶Fear seized all of them; and they glorified God, saying, "A great prophet has risen among us!" and "God has looked favorably on his people!" ¹⁷This word about him spread throughout Judea and all the surrounding country.

> The importance of resurrection stories in the gospels is to foreshadow the central message of Christianity, the death and resurrection of Jesus.
>
> —Alfred McBride, OPraem, *The Kingdom and the Glory: Meditation and Commentary on the Gospel of Matthew*

¹⁸ The disciples of John reported all these things to him. So John summoned two of his disciples ¹⁹and sent them to the Lord to ask, "Are you the one who is to come, or are we to wait for another?" ²⁰When the men had come to him, they said, "John the Baptist has sent us to you to ask, 'Are you the one who is to come or are we to wait for another?'" ²¹Jesus had just then cured many people of diseases, plagues, and evil spirits, and had given sight to many who were blind. ²²And he answered them, "Go and tell John what you have seen and heard: the blind receive their sight, the lame walk, the lepers are cleansed, the deaf hear, the dead are raised, the poor have good news brought to them. ²³And blessed is anyone who takes no offense at me."

As Jesus and his followers approached Nain, a town lying to the southwest of the Sea of Galilee, they met a procession of mourners accompanying a widow who was about to bury her only son. Shortly before, Jesus had healed a man so ill that he had been about to die (Luke 7:2-10). Now, in a scene charged with dramatic intensity, the Lord—the "Author of life" (Acts 3:15)—encountered a man already dead and showed his power over death.

Jesus was moved with compassion at the sight of the weeping mother. *Esplanchnisthe*, the Greek expression Luke used to describe Jesus' feeling, means "to be filled with heartfelt mercy," "to have mercy from one's inner core." Jesus' heart went out to the woman in her painful loss, and he recognized the hardship of her situation, as well. Without husband and son, she had no male protector and provider, no economic security. Without any means of earning a living, she would be solely dependent on the charity of others. Seeing her grief and need, Jesus immediately acted on her behalf.

Since burying the dead was a meritorious work of mercy (Tobit 1:17; Sirach 38:16-17), friends and neighbors of the woman and her son, townspeople, and perhaps even hired mourners and musicians would have been part of the funeral procession. Jesus halted the procession by touching the bier, and probably signaled to the bearers to set the bier down. Then, taking everyone by surprise, he said, "Young man, I say to you, rise!" (Luke 7:14). The words Jesus spoke were a command addressed directly to the corpse, not a prayer for the deceased addressed to God. At this command, the dead man sat up and spoke (7:15). Just as sickness, the forces of nature, and Satan had submitted to Jesus' authority on so many other occasions, death now submitted, too.

Faith was not required of anyone for this miracle—no one had asked or expected Jesus to raise the young man—but the miracle inspired faith. Those who witnessed the dead man's restoration glorified God and hailed Jesus as a great prophet through whom God was acting (Luke 7:16).

The raising of the young man of Nain was a sign of the advent of the messianic age and pointed to Jesus as "the one who is to come" (Luke 7:19). This miraculous event anticipated Jesus' reply to the messengers sent by John the Baptist to inquire about his identity: "Go and tell John what you have seen and heard: the blind receive their sight, the lame walk, the lepers are cleansed, the deaf hear, the dead are raised, the poor have good news brought to them" (7:22; see also Isaiah 29:18-19; 35:5-6). Jesus' miracle was prefigured in the Old Testament account of Elijah's restoring the son of the widow of Zarephath to life (1 Kings 17:17-24; see also Luke 4:26). Yet whereas Elijah was a great prophet who prayed to God to revive the child, Jesus restored the young man's life himself—because he is the Lord of creation, Author of life, and Messiah.

> The miracle in Nain points to Jesus' ultimate victory over death.

Finally, the miracle in Nain points to Jesus' ultimate victory over death and is "an epiphany of the glory of Jesus that will be fully manifested in his own resurrection" (René Latourelle, *The Miracles of Jesus and the Theology of Miracles*). Jesus restored life to the widow's son (Luke 7:11-17), Lazarus (John 11:38-44), and Jairus' daughter (Matthew 9:18-19, 23-25; Mark 5:35-42; Luke 8:49-55)—but that life, though renewed, was still mortal, and each of those people would die again. Jesus' own rising from the dead was a resurrection to true immortality. And in the final resurrection, when "this perishable body puts on imperishability, and this mortal body puts on immortality" (1 Corinthians 15:54), we will live with him for all eternity.

Understand!

1. What does the miracle in Nain reveal about Jesus' divine nature? About his human character? What other instances in the gospels can you recall when Jesus was moved by compassion?

_____

_____

_____

_____

_____

_____

2. Occasionally Jesus effected a miracle by his touch or through some other physical action; in other instances he simply spoke a word. In this case, he did both. What does this suggest to you about his power? About his authority?

_____

_____

_____

_____

_____

_____

3. Describe the stages of the crowd's reaction when the dead man sat up and spoke (Luke 7:16-17). How might the response of those who witnessed this miracle have affected other people?

_____

_____

_____

_____

_____

_____

4. What characteristics of Jesus' messianic mission can you identify in this event? What does this event indicate about the nature of the kingdom of God?

_____

_____

_____

_____

_____

_____

5. Read 1 Kings 17:17-24. What similarities do you find between this account of Elijah's raising a child from the dead and Luke's account of Jesus' raising the young man in Nain? What differences? What do these differences add to your conception and understanding of Jesus?

_____

_____

_____

_____

_____

_____

▶ In the Spotlight
Wisdom from the Church Fathers

The Virgin's son met the widow's son. He became like a sponge for her tears and as life for the death of her son. Death turned about in its den and turned its back on the victorious one.
—**St. Ephrem**, *Commentary on Tatian's Diatessaron*

The widowed mother rejoiced at the raising of that young man. Our Mother the Church rejoices every day when people are raised again in spirit. The young man had been dead physically; the latter, dead spiritually. The young man's death

was mourned visibly; the death of the latter was invisible and unmourned. He seeks them out Who knew them to be dead; only he can bring them back to life.
—St. Augustine, *Sermon 98*

What is more powerful than the Word of God? Why then did he not work the miracle by only a word but also touched the bier? It was, my beloved, that you might learn that the holy body of Christ is productive for the salvation of man. The flesh of the almighty Word is the body of life and was clothed with his might. Consider that iron when brought into contact with fire produces the effects of fire and fulfills its functions. The flesh of Christ also has the power of giving life and annihilates the influence of death and corruption because it is the flesh of the Word, who gives life to all. May our Lord Jesus Christ also touch us that delivering us from evil works, even from fleshly lusts, he may unite us to the assemblies of saints.
—St. Cyril of Alexandria, *Commentary on Luke*

Grow!

1. Jesus showed compassion to the woman even though she had made no request to him. Are you willing to accept the free gift of God's mercy? Why or why not? How do you react to God's initiative in your life, especially when you haven't asked for it?

_____

_____

_____

_____

_____

_____

2. Is there any area of your life that seems to be "dead" and in need of renewal or restoration right now? If so, write a prayer telling Jesus of this need and of your desire to hear him say to you, "Rise!"

_____

_____

_____

_____

_____

_____

_____

3. Jesus comforted the widow, telling her, "Do not weep" (Luke 7:13). What words of compassion or comfort has Jesus ever spoken to you? How did they affect your relationship with him?

_____

_____

_____

_____

_____

_____

4. Imagine yourself among the crowd that witnessed this resurrection. How do you think you might have reacted? Is it difficult for you to believe that Jesus still acts miraculously in the world today? Do you have difficulty believing in the future resurrection? Why or why not?

_____

_____

_____

_____

_____

_____

5. What aspect of this miracle account is most striking to you? Why? What impact has it made on you?

_____

_____

_____

_____

_____

_____

_____

▶ In the Spotlight
Kyrios

Kyrios is the title used in the Greek version of the Old Testament to translate God's personal name—"Yahweh" or "I AM"—from Hebrew. In English it is rendered as "the Lord."

This title, which is commonly attributed to Jesus throughout the New Testament, is the most exalted one of all those given to him, because as Scripture commentator Stephen Binz notes, it refers "to his risen glory and his sovereign authority at the right hand of his Father. . . . [W]hen the followers of Jesus proclaimed him as Lord, they were implying that Jesus shared in the authority and divinity of the God of Israel. To call Jesus 'the Lord' is to praise him as the mighty presence of God come to dwell among us" (Stephen Binz, *The Names of Jesus*).

Kyrios appears for the first time in Luke's gospel in this narrative of the raising of the young man in Nain: "When the Lord [*Kyrios*] saw her, he had compassion for her and said to her, 'Do not weep'" (Luke 7:13). The use of *Kyrios* is yet another indication that the messianic age has come.

Reflect!

1. Reflect on these words of fifth-century monk and bishop St. Paulinus of Nola:

   > It is a loving act to show sadness when our dear ones are torn from us, but it is a holy act to be joyful through hope and trust in the promises of God. . . . Granted our love may weep for a time, but our faith must ever rejoice. We should long for those who have been sent before us, but we should not lose hope of gaining them back. (*The Quotable Saint*)

   How do you express your grief and sympathy as well as your faith and hope in God to someone who has lost a loved one? How could you grow in greater compassion and sensitivity toward those who are suffering loss?

2. Reflect on the following Scripture passages to deepen your appreciation of Jesus' resurrection and your hope in the resurrection to come:

   > [O]n the first day of the week, at early dawn, they came to the tomb, taking the spices that they had prepared. They found the stone rolled away from the tomb, but when they went in, they did not find the body. While they were perplexed about this, suddenly two men in dazzling clothes stood beside them. The women were terrified and bowed their faces to the ground, but the men said to them, "Why do you look for the living among the dead? He is not here, but has risen."
   >
   > —Luke 24:1-6

Martha said to Jesus, "Lord, if you had been here, my brother [Lazarus] would not have died. But even now I know that God will give you whatever you ask of him." Jesus said to her, "Your brother will rise again." Martha said to him, "I know that he will rise again in the resurrection on the last day." Jesus said to her, "I am the resurrection and the life. Those who believe in me, even though they die, will live, and everyone who lives and believes in me will never die."

—John 11:21-26

Peter, standing with the eleven, raised his voice and addressed them, . . . "You that are Israelites, listen to what I have to say: Jesus of Nazareth, a man attested to you by God with deeds of power, wonders, and signs that God did through him among you, as you yourselves know—this man, handed over to you according to the definite plan and foreknowledge of God, you crucified and killed by the hands of those outside the law. But God raised him up, having freed him from death, because it was impossible for him to be held in its power."

—Acts 2:14, 22-24

Listen, I will tell you a mystery! We will not all die, but we will all be changed, in a moment, in the twinkling of an eye, at the last trumpet. For the trumpet will sound, and the dead will be raised imperishable, and we will be changed. For this perishable body must put on imperishability, and this mortal body must put on immortality. When this perishable body puts on imperishability, and this mortal body puts on immortality, then the saying that is written will be fulfilled: "Death has been swallowed up in victory."

—1 Corinthians 15:51-54

[T]he Lord himself, with a cry of command, with the archangel's call and with the sound of God's trumpet, will descend from heaven, and the dead in Christ will rise first. Then we who are alive, who are left, will be caught up in the clouds together with them to meet the Lord in the air; and so we will be with the Lord forever. Therefore encourage one another with these words.

—1 Thessalonians 4:16-18

▶ In the Spotlight
Contemporary Voices

The hope generated by the resurrection of Christ, proclaimed in Luke 7:11-17, contradicts suffering and death experienced in so many ways in everyday life. Suffering, evil, injustice, death are experienced by people as abandonment by God, remoteness of God. The hope of the resurrection, founded on God's fidelity to his promise, announces the proximity of God, the victory of life over death. To the Christian death remains real, but it loses its fatal character. God has raised Jesus, and in his victory over death ours is included as the promise of our faithful God who has visited his people in and through Jesus.
—**Herman Hendrickx, CICM,** *The Miracle Stories of the Synoptic Gospels*

This incident . . . shows the Evangelist's special delight in portraying Jesus not only overwhelmed with pity at the sight of tragedy but also turning with kindly regard toward women.
—**Carroll Stuhlmueller, CP,** *The Gospel According to Luke*

Act!

Christian martyrs witness boldly to their faith in Jesus as the Son of God and their faith in the resurrection. Millions of men and women have willingly suffered and died rather than deny their Savior. They believed that in death, they were not losers but victors, for "the sufferings of this present time are not worth comparing with the glory about to be revealed to us" (Romans 8:18).

This week read an account of one of the Christian martyrs. Pay special attention to how, in the face of death, belief and hope in the resurrection are a source of strength and consolation.

▶ In the Spotlight
The Tenderness of the Heart of Christ

Jesus crosses paths again with a crowd of people. He could have passed by or waited until they called him. But he didn't. He took the initiative because he was moved by a widow's sorrow. She had just lost all she had, her son.

The evangelist explains that Jesus was moved. Perhaps he even showed signs of it, as when Lazarus died. Jesus Christ was not, and is not, insensitive to the suffering that stems from love. He is pained at seeing children separated from their parents. He overcomes death so as to give life, to reunite those who love one another. But at the same time, he requires that we first admit the preeminence of divine love, which alone can inspire genuine Christian living.

Christ knows he is surrounded by a crowd which will be awed by the miracle and will tell the story all over the countryside.

But he does not act artificially, merely to create an effect. Quite simply he is touched by that woman's suffering and cannot but console her. So he goes up to her and says, "Do not weep." It is like saying, "I don't want to see you crying; I have come on earth to bring joy and peace." And then comes the miracle, the sign of the power of Christ who is God. But first came his compassion, an evident sign of the tenderness of the heart of Christ the man.

—St. Josemaría Escrivá, *Christ Is Passing By*

"All Ate and Were Filled"

Mark 6:30-44

³⁰ The apostles gathered around Jesus, and told him all that they had done and taught. ³¹He said to them, "Come away to a deserted place all by yourselves and rest a while." For many were coming and going, and they had no leisure even to eat. ³²And they went away in the boat to a deserted place by themselves. ³³Now many saw them going and recognized them, and they hurried there on foot from all the towns and arrived ahead of them. ³⁴As he went ashore, he saw a great crowd; and he had compassion for them, because they were like sheep without a shepherd; and he began to teach them many things. ³⁵When it grew late, his disciples came to him and said, "This is a deserted place, and the hour is now very late; ³⁶send them away so that they may go into the surrounding country and villages and buy something for themselves to eat." ³⁷But he answered them, "You give them something to eat." They said to him, "Are we to go and buy two hundred denarii worth of bread, and give it to them to eat?" ³⁸And he said to them, "How many loaves have you? Go and see." When they had found out, they said, "Five, and two fish." ³⁹Then he ordered them to get all the people to sit down in groups on the green grass. ⁴⁰So they sat down in groups of hundreds and of fifties. ⁴¹Taking the five loaves and the two fish, he looked up to heaven, and blessed and broke the loaves, and gave them to his disciples to set before the people; and he divided the two fish among them all. ⁴²And all ate and were filled; ⁴³and they took up twelve baskets full of broken pieces and of the fish. ⁴⁴Those who had eaten the loaves numbered five thousand men.

(See also Matthew 14:13-21; 15:32-39; Luke 9:10-17; and John 6:1-14)

> Jesus ordered that the fragments be gathered up; they filled twelve baskets. In the reckoning of men there is always a deficit; in the arithmetic of God, there is always a surplus.
> —Archbishop Fulton J. Sheen, *Life of Christ*

J esus had "appointed twelve, whom he also named apostles, to be with him, and to be sent out to proclaim the message, and to have authority to cast out demons" (Mark 3:14-15). They had been busy sharing in Jesus' ministry, preaching repentance and even healing the sick (6:12-13), and now they had returned, eager to tell Jesus all they had done. Tired from the continual press and clamor of the crowds, Jesus sought a place of rest for himself and the twelve (6:30-32). It was futile, however. When Jesus was recognized, the people hurried after him (6:33).

Rather than become aggravated at the vast company who were "like sheep without a shepherd" (Mark 6:34), Jesus once again showed great compassion. "In his own body God has felt the hunger of the poor, their thirst, their exhaustion," wrote François Mauriac in his renowned *Life of Jesus*. "He has had a part in their sweat, their tears, their blood." First Jesus taught the crowd in order to satisfy their spiritual hunger (6:34). Then, recognizing how late it had become and how long it must have been since they had last eaten, Jesus fed their physical hunger too.

Trying to feed so many people didn't make sense to the apostles (Mark 6:37). As they logically pointed out, not even two hundred days' wages could have bought enough food for such a crowd! They focused on what was lacking, and the magnitude of the need hindered their faith. Like Jesus' disciples, we often think that the bigger the problem, the less likely it can be overcome! But Jesus was not deterred by the size of the crowd or the meagerness of the provisions at hand. Rather, he blessed the few loaves and fish that could be found—most likely with the traditional Jewish prayer, "Blessed are you, Lord our God, king of the universe, who bring forth bread from the earth." With this act of thanksgiving, in which he acknowledged the gift of the Father, Jesus opened the way for the miracle he performed.

Just as God had miraculously fed the Israelites with manna—"bread from heaven"—and quail when they hungered in the desert (Exodus 16:1-15), Jesus now showed his divine power and fed the hungry crowd with a miraculous quantity of bread and fish. In Jesus' actions we see a foreshadowing of the Last Supper and the Eucharist—"the bread of life" (John 6:35). This feeding of the five thousand also anticipates the great banquet—"a feast of rich food" (Isaiah 25:6)—that will occur when Jesus returns at the end of time to invite us to "the marriage supper of the Lamb" (Revelation 19:9; see also Matthew 8:11).

The disciples must have been incredulous at first and then humbled as they distributed the few loaves of bread and fish, only to find more every time they reached into the basket. The five thousand people received not just a mouthful each, but were "filled" (Mark 6:42). As with the abundance of wine at Cana (John 2:6), Jesus was not stinting with the quantity of food he provided. Nor was anything of God's abundance to be wasted. "Gather up the fragments left over, so that nothing may be lost," he said (6:12). The twelve baskets full of pieces of broken bread and fish may allude to the twelve apostles, who represent the foundations of the church, or to the twelve tribes of Israel.

> Jesus' miraculous multiplication of the loaves and fish calls us to faith in him as the Son of God. It is also an invitation and a challenge to place our trust in his deep love for us.

Jesus' miraculous multiplication of the loaves and fish calls us to faith in him as the Son of God. It is also an invitation and a challenge to place our trust in his deep love for us—love made manifest in his daily care for us and in the Eucharist, his body given to nourish and strengthen us on our journey to heaven.

Understand!

1. What demands of Jesus' ministry in Galilee are depicted in this gospel scene? See also Mark 3:19b-20. What effect did these demands have on Jesus and his disciples? How did he respond to these conditions?

_____

_____

_____

_____

_____

2. What does the disciples' exchange with Jesus in Mark 6:35-37 indicate to you about them? What does it suggest about their relationship with Jesus and their understanding of him?

_____

_____

_____

_____

_____

3. Compare Jesus' actions and gestures in Mark 6:41 with those described in Mark 14:22 and Luke 24:30. In what ways does the multiplication of the loaves prefigure the Eucharist?

_____

_____

_____

_____

_____

4. What possible reasons could Jesus have had for asking the disciples to distribute the bread and fish? (Mark 6:41; see also Matthew 14:19; 15:36; Luke 9:16). What effect might this miracle have had on the disciples?

_____

_____

_____

_____

_____

_____

5. What significance do you see in the quantity of leftovers? Why do you think Jesus multiplied the loaves and fish to such an excess?

_____

_____

_____

_____

_____

_____

▶ In the Spotlight
Wisdom from the Church Fathers

This bread which Jesus breaks is truly the mystical Word of God and a discourse about Christ which is increased while it is distributed. From a few discourses, he ministered abundant nourishment to all peoples. He gave discourses to us like loaves that are doubled when they are poured forth from our mouths. That bread in an incomprehensible fashion is visibly increased when it is broken, when it is distributed, when it is eaten without any understanding of how it is provided. . . . Truly, Christ's gifts seem small but are very great. They are not bestowed on one person but on peoples, for the food grew

in the mouth of those who ate it. This food seemed to be for bodily nourishment but was taken for eternal salvation.
—St. Ambrose, *Exposition of the Gospel of Luke*

There were also gathered twelve baskets of fragments. And what do we infer from this? A plain assurance that hospitality receives a rich recompense from God. The disciples offered five loaves. After a multitude this large had been satisfied, there was gathered for each of them a basketful of fragments. Let nothing, therefore, prevent willing people from receiving strangers, no matter what there may be likely to blunt the will and readiness of men. Let no one say, "I do not possess suitable means. What I can do is altogether trifling and insufficient for many." Receive strangers, my beloved. Overcome that reluctance which wins no reward. The Savior will multiply the little you have many times beyond expectation. Although you give but little, you will receive much. For he that sows blessings shall also reap blessings, according to the blessed Paul's words (2 Corinthians 9:6).
—St. Cyril of Alexandria, *Commentary on Luke*

Grow!

1. In what ways has Jesus asked you to share in his work? When has he sent you out on a mission as he sent out the twelve (Mark 3:14-15; 6:7, 12-13)? What happened? What impact did this have on your faith and trust in God?

_____

_____

_____

_____

_____

2. When have you shown compassion to a person who was "hungry" in some way? What makes you sometimes unwilling to let your "rest time" be interrupted by those in need?

_____

_____

_____

_____

_____

_____

3. How do you feel when the needs you see around you far exceed your natural ability to meet them? Are you able to give the little you have in faith, believing that God can use you and what you have to offer?

_____

_____

_____

_____

_____

_____

4. In what area of your life are you aware of having only a meager "five loaves and two fish"? What would you like to see God multiply in your life? A personal limitation? A talent or skill? Your love for God? Your compassion toward others?

_____

_____

_____

_____

_____

_____

5. It was as the bread and fish were broken and given away that they were multiplied. What might God be asking you to "break" or give over to him? How could this allow you to be of greater benefit to others?

_____

_____

_____

_____

_____

▶ In the Spotlight
God's Tender Care

We cook for 9,000 people every day. One day one Sister came and said, "Mother, there's nothing to eat, nothing to give to the people." I had no answer. And then by 9:00 that morning a truck full of bread came to our house. The government gives a slice of bread and milk to the poor children. That day—no one in the city knew why—but suddenly all the schools were closed. And all the bread came to Mother Teresa. See, God closed the schools. He would not let our people go without food. And this was the first time, I think, in their lives that they had such good bread and so much. This way you can see the tenderness of God.

—Blessed Mother Teresa of Calcutta, *Jesus, the Word to be Spoken*

Reflect!

1. Think about how you approach the table of the Lord at Mass. Do your outward actions and posture correspond to the inward disposition of your heart when you receive Communion? How

might you better prepare to receive Jesus in the Eucharist and offer thanks to him afterward? (The Greek verb for "give thanks" is *eucharisteo*, which gives us the word "Eucharist.")

2. Reflect on the following Scripture passages to enhance your understanding of the Eucharist and your appreciation for it:

> [I]n the morning there was a layer of dew around the camp. When the layer of dew lifted, there on the surface of the wilderness was a fine flaky substance, as fine as frost on the ground. When the Israelites saw it, they said to one another, "What is it?" For they did not know what it was. Moses said to them, "It is the bread that the LORD has given you to eat." . . . The house of Israel called it manna; it was like coriander seed, white, and the taste of it was like wafers made with honey. . . . The Israelites ate manna forty years, until they came to a habitable land; they ate manna, until they came to the border of the land of Canaan.
>
> —Exodus 16:13-15, 31, 35

> [H]e commanded the skies above,
>   and opened the doors of heaven;
> he rained down on them manna to eat,
>   and gave them the grain of heaven.
> Mortals ate of the bread of angels;
>   he sent them food in abundance.
>   —Psalm 78:23-25

> While they were eating, Jesus took a loaf of bread, and after blessing it he broke it, gave it to the disciples, and said, "Take, eat; this is my body." Then he took a cup, and after giving thanks he gave it to them, saying, "Drink

from it, all of you; for this is my blood of the covenant, which is poured out for many for the forgiveness of sins."

—Matthew 26:26-28

Then Jesus said to them, "Very truly, I tell you, it was not Moses who gave you the bread from heaven, but it is my Father who gives you the true bread from heaven. For the bread of God is that which comes down from heaven and gives life to the world." They said to him, "Sir, give us this bread always." Jesus said to them, "I am the bread of life. Whoever comes to me will never be hungry, and whoever believes in me will never be thirsty. . . . I am the bread of life. Your ancestors ate the manna in the wilderness, and they died. This is the bread that comes down from heaven, so that one may eat of it and not die. I am the living bread that came down from heaven. Whoever eats of this bread will live forever; and the bread that I will give for the life of the world is my flesh."

—John 6:32-35, 48-51

For I [Paul] received from the Lord what I also handed on to you, that the Lord Jesus on the night when he was betrayed took a loaf of bread, and when he had given thanks, he broke it, and said, "This is my body that is for you. Do this in remembrance of me." In the same way he took the cup also, after supper, saying, "This cup is the new covenant in my blood. Do this, as often as you drink it, in remembrance of me." For as often as you eat this bread and drink the cup, you proclaim the Lord's death until he comes.

—1 Corinthians 11:23-26

▶ In the Spotlight
Medicine of Immortality

Francis Xavier Nguyen Van Thuan was appointed coadjutor bishop of Saigon (Ho Chi Minh City) in 1974 and a few months later was arrested by Vietnam's Communist government. After spending thirteen years in various prisons and three years under house arrest, he was expelled from Vietnam. He went to Rome, where he served in the Roman Curia and was named a cardinal by Pope John Paul II in 2001. Cardinal Nguyen Van Thuan died of cancer in 2002.

When I was arrested, I had to leave immediately with empty hands. The next day, I was permitted to write to my people in order to ask for the most necessary things: clothes, toothpaste. . . . I wrote, "Please send me a little wine as medicine for my stomachache." The faithful understood right away.

They sent me a small bottle of wine for Mass with a label that read, "medicine for stomachaches." They also sent some hosts, which they hid in a flashlight for protection against the humidity. . . .

I will never be able to express my great joy! Every day, with three drops of wine and a drop of water in the palm of my hand, I would celebrate Mass. This was my altar, and this was my cathedral! It was true medicine for the soul and body, "Medicine of immortality, remedy so as not to die but to have life always in Jesus," as St. Ignatius of Antioch says. . . .

So, for many years I was nourished with the bread of life and the cup of salvation. . . . The Eucharist became for me and for the other Christians a hidden and encouraging presence in the midst of all our difficulties. Jesus was adored secretly by the

Christians who lived with me, just as happened so often in other prison camps of the twentieth century.

In the re-education camp, we were divided into groups of fifty people; we slept on a common bed, and everyone had a right to 50 centimeters of space. We managed to make sure that there were five Catholics with me. At 9:30 p.m. we had to turn off the lights and everyone had to go to sleep. It was then that I would bow over the bed to celebrate the Mass by heart, and I distributed communion by passing my hand under the mosquito net. We even made little sacks from the paper of cigarette packs to preserve the Most Holy Sacrament and bring it to others. The Eucharistic Jesus was always with me in my shirt pocket.

Every week there was an indoctrination session in which the whole camp had to participate. My Catholic companions and I took advantage of the breaks in order to pass the small sack to everyone in the four other groups of prisoners. Everyone knew that Jesus was in their midst. At night, the prisoners would take turns for adoration. With his silent presence, the Eucharistic Jesus helped us in unimaginable ways. Many Christians returned to a fervent faith-life, and their witness of service and love had an ever greater impact on the other prisoners. Even Buddhists and other non-Christians came to the faith. The strength of Jesus' love was irresistible.
—**Cardinal Francis Xavier Nguyen Van Thuan,**
Testimony of Hope

Act!

"Break your bread" and see it "multiplied" this week.

Donate food to a local food bank, visit an elderly friend, volunteer at a soup kitchen, invite a lonely neighbor to dinner, share a talent or skill. Give your time, energy, talents, and/or financial resources and allow God to put them to use for the benefit of others.

▶ In the Spotlight
In the Words of the Saints

Every day [Jesus] humbles Himself just as He did when He came from His heavenly throne into the Virgin's womb; every day He comes to us and lets us see Him in lowliness, when He descends from the bosom of the Father into the hands of the priest at the altar.
—**St. Francis of Assisi**

Jesus Christ found a way by which he could ascend into Heaven and yet remain on the earth. He instituted the adorable Sacrament of the Eucharist so that he might stay with us and be the Food for our soul; that he might stay with us and be our Companion.
—**St. John Vianney**

Our Savior has instituted the most august sacrament of the Eucharist, which contains his flesh and blood in their reality, so that whoever eats of it shall live forever. Therefore, whoever turns to it frequently and devoutly so effectively builds up his soul's health that it is almost impossible for him to be poisoned by evil affection of any kind.
—**St. Francis de Sales**

"Jesus, Master, Have Mercy!"

Luke 17:11-19

¹¹ On the way to Jerusalem Jesus was going through the region between Samaria and Galilee. ¹²As he entered a village, ten lepers approached him. Keeping their distance, ¹³they called out, saying, "Jesus, Master, have mercy on us." ¹⁴When he saw them, he said to them, "Go and show yourselves to the priests." And as they went, they were made clean. ¹⁵Then one of them, when he saw that he was healed, turned back, praising God with a loud voice. ¹⁶He prostrated himself at Jesus' feet and thanked him. And he was a Samaritan. ¹⁷Then Jesus asked, "Were not ten made clean? But the other nine, where are they? ¹⁸Was none of them found to return and give praise to God except this foreigner?" ¹⁹Then he said to him, "Get up and go on your way; your faith has made you well."

Gratitude makes us see the good. When we are grateful, we acknowledge that we are indebted, that we have received more than we deserve. . . . What we need is to have some "Samaritan" in us; what we need is to follow our natural instinct to be grateful. The first characteristic of the Christian is to be grateful.

—**Archbishop Marcel Gervais**, *Homily at Notre Dame Cathedral, Ottawa*

Leprosy was a dreaded disease in biblical times. Besides suffering physical disability and disfigurement, a person afflicted with leprosy was considered ritually unclean and was forbidden to come into contact with people who were healthy (Leviticus 13:45-46). Segregated from society, those suffering from leprosy lived on the outskirts of towns and begged for alms, relying on charity for their survival.

The ten whom Jesus healed in the gospel story were drawn together by their common affliction. Since Jews despised Samaritans as apostates—people who rejected the faith—the two groups usually avoided each other (2 Kings 17:24-41; Matthew 10:5; Luke 9:52-55; John 4:9). But in the desperation of their condition, these people ignored this customary animosity and shared a fellowship of suffering.

Conscious of their "uncleanness" and the risk of transmitting their contagious disease, the ten were careful not to approach Jesus too closely when they cried, "Master, have mercy on us" (Luke 17:13). The distance they kept, however, presented no barrier to Jesus' compassion and power.

Jesus didn't heal these people on the spot; instead, he commanded them to show themselves to the priests (Luke 17:14). Mosaic law stipulated that a cure of leprosy had to be certified by the priests (Leviticus 14:1-32)—in this way, a person was declared clean and was no longer a social outcast. Sensitive to every aspect of their pain, Jesus' intent was not only to restore these people to health but also to ensure that they would be fully restored to normal society by officially receiving a "clean bill of health."

Perhaps this group of people had heard about the wonders Jesus was performing throughout Galilee; their cry for mercy was filled with expectant faith. If they already believed that he could make them whole again, they may have left Jesus filled with rising hopes and confidence. Or, still marked by the ravages of their disease, they may have departed with disappointment, wondering how the priests would respond to them. In any case, it was only after they went on their way, obeying Jesus' directive, that they were cured (Luke 17:14).

As soon as one of the ten—a Samaritan (Luke 17:16)—became aware of his healing, he raced back to Jesus, loudly praising God (17:15). No waiting for a more convenient moment for him! He simply couldn't let the master go without thanking him right away. And when the Samaritan found Jesus, he threw himself at his feet (17:16)—the proper place to humbly acknowledge how undeserving he was of God's mercy and to give thanks. Surely such an expression of gratitude brought Jesus great pleasure.

Jesus' healing of the Samaritan recalls the prophet Elisha's encounter in Samaria with Naaman, a foreigner who also suffered from leprosy (2 Kings 5:1-14). Initially Naaman balked at Elisha's command to wash in the Jordan River, but when he eventually obeyed the prophet, "his flesh was restored like the flesh of a young boy, and he was clean" (5:14). He returned from the river to thank Elisha for his cure and honored the God of Israel (5:15). Naaman's cleansing through water is a type of baptism. The story also points toward the adoption of foreigners into God's covenant and the universality of salvation (Isaiah 56:3-8). Similarly, the gospel account of the leprous Samaritan's faith is a prelude to the influx of many Samaritans into the church through the preaching of the apostles following Jesus' resurrection (Acts 8:5-8, 14-17, 25).

Jesus' final words to the Samaritan—"your faith has made you well" (Luke 17:19)—echo his message to the woman he cured of a hemorrhage (8:48). Like her, the grateful man was given far more than physical well-being. Through his faith and obedience, he had received wholeness of body and spirit, peace, and friendship with God in Christ.

Understand!

1. With what attitude do you think the ten people with leprosy approached Jesus? What does Jesus' command to them suggest to you about the relationship between obedience and faith? Did Jesus always require that those he healed have faith?

_____

_____

_____

_____

_____

_____

2. List the verbs that describe the Samaritan's successive actions in response to his healing (Luke 17:15-16). What do these actions say about the man's relationship to God? Think of others in the gospels who prostrated themselves at the feet of Jesus—for example, the Syrophoenician woman (Mark 7:25-26), Jairus (Luke 8:41-42), and Mary of Bethany (John 11:32; 12:3). What did they express by their posture?

_____

_____

_____

_____

_____

_____

3. Jesus asked the Samaritan, "Were not ten made clean? But the other nine, where are they? Was none of them found to return and give praise to God except this foreigner?" (Luke 17:17-18). In what tone of voice do you think he asked these questions?

Why? What do Jesus' questions add to your understanding of him? Of his relationship with the Father?

_____

_____

_____

_____

_____

_____

_____

4. Why was it significant that it was "this foreigner" (Luke 17:18) who gave thanks to God? What does the Samaritan's presence in this story indicate about Jesus' mission? About Jesus himself?

_____

_____

_____

_____

_____

_____

_____

5. What similarities do you see in the healing of the ten people with leprosy and the healing of the paralyzed man (Luke 5:17-26)? What differences? What do the differences as well as the similarities suggest to you about Jesus, the Great Physician?

_____

_____

_____

_____

_____

_____

_____

It is evident from the whole teaching of scripture that the Lord loves to be thanked and praised just as much as we do. I am sure that it gives him real downright pleasure, just as it does us and that our failure to thank him for his gifts wounds his loving heart, just as our hearts are wounded when our loved ones fail to appreciate the benefits we have so enjoyed bestowing on them. What joy it is to receive from our friends an acknowledgment of their thanksgiving for our gifts, and is it not likely that it is a joy to the Lord also?
—**Hannah Whitall Smith,** *Daily He Leads Me*

Grow!

1. In ancient times, leprosy was considered incurable, yet Jesus miraculously healed ten people afflicted by the disease. What sin or difficulty in your life do you consider to be "incurable," hopeless, impossible to overcome or change? How free do you feel to cry out to the Lord in your need? What hinders you or limits your faith and expectation?

_____

_____

_____

_____

_____

_____

_____

2. The ten people who came to Jesus to be cured acted on his command to show themselves to the priests without any proof or assurance of what the results would be. Think of an occasion

when you stepped forth in faith, obeying Jesus' word. What happened? What effect did this have on you?

_____

_____

_____

_____

_____

_____

_____

_____

3. The Samaritan thanked Jesus by praising him in a loud voice and falling at his feet (Luke 17:15-16). How could your actions, as well as your words, give thanks to God?

_____

_____

_____

_____

_____

_____

_____

4. How does a sense of gratitude to God change us and our outlook on a situation? What happens when we fail to acknowledge God's generosity?

_____

_____

_____

_____

_____

_____

_____

5. Think of someone you know who is ill, lonely, suffering from a mental or physical limitation, or is in some way "marginalized" or cut off from society. What is one thing you could do this week to make them feel less isolated and more connected to the body of Christ?

_____

_____

_____

_____

_____

▶ In the Spotlight
Hansen's Disease

Leprosy is a chronic infectious disease that mainly affects the eyes, skin, peripheral nerves, and mucous membranes of the upper respiratory tract. It was known in ancient Egypt, Israel, India, China, Greece, and Rome. In the Middle Ages leprosy also spread rapidly across Europe. There was little palliative treatment for the disease and no hope for a cure. To protect the populace from contagion, strict laws were enacted that banned those afflicted with the disease from all social contact. As a consequence, in addition to their physical afflictions, leprosy sufferers also bore the stigma of being "outcasts," rejected and excluded from society. By the fifteenth century leprosy had declined in Europe, but the disease is still common in India, Brazil, Myanmar (Burma), Indonesia, Nepal, Madagascar, Ethiopia, Mozambique, Tanzania, and the Democratic Republic of the Congo.

In 1873 a Norwegian doctor, Gerhard Hansen, first identified the bacillus of leprosy, _Mycobacterium leprae_. Today leprosy is curable with Multidrug Therapy (MDT), a powerful combination of clofazimine, rifampicin, and dapsone. Once treatment begins, the disease's advance in the body is halted and the patient is no longer contagious. At the beginning of 2005, approximately 300,000 leprosy patients were under active treatment worldwide.

Ten million leprosy patients have been cured during the past fifteen years. Nonetheless, Hansen's disease, as leprosy is now called, still remains a serious illness. Currently, an estimated two to four million people around the world have been so visibly and irreversibly disabled by leprosy that they require ongoing care.

Reflect!

1. Examine your heart. Ask the Holy Spirit to reveal to you any attitudes—for example, discontentment, taking God's benefits for granted, holding on to your own agenda, complacency—that blind you to God's blessings and block you from experiencing and expressing gratitude. What could you do to overcome such hindrances and change your outlook? To make giving thanks to God a more conscious and active part of your life?

2. Reflect on the following Scripture passages that portray expressions of gratitude to God for his goodness and gifts:

> [David] appointed certain of the Levites as ministers before the ark of the LORD, to invoke, to thank, and to praise the LORD, the God of Israel. Asaph . . . was to sound the cymbals, and the priests Benaiah and Jahaziel were to blow trumpets regularly, before the ark of the covenant of God. Then on that day David first appointed the singing of praises to the LORD by Asaph and his kindred.
> —1 Chronicles 16:4, 5b-7

It is good to give thanks to the LORD,
>to sing praises to your name, O Most High;
to declare your steadfast love in the morning,
>and your faithfulness by night,
to the music of the lute and the harp,
>to the melody of the lyre.
For you, O LORD, have made me glad
>>by your work;
>at the works of your hands I sing for joy.
>>>>—Psalm 92:1-4

Bless the LORD, O my soul,
>and all that is within me,
>bless his holy name.
Bless the LORD, O my soul,
>and do not forget all his benefits—
who forgives all your iniquity,
>who heals all your diseases,
who redeems your life from the Pit,
>who crowns you with steadfast love and mercy,
who satisfies you with good as long as you live
>so that your youth is renewed like the eagle's.
>>>>—Psalm 103:1-5

[B]e filled with the Spirit, as you sing psalms and hymns and spiritual songs among yourselves, singing and making melody to the Lord in your hearts, giving thanks to God the Father at all times and for everything in the name of our Lord Jesus Christ.

>>>>—Ephesians 5:18-20

What better words may we carry in our heart, pronounce with our mouth, write with a pen, than the words, "Thanks be to God"? There is no phrase that may be said so readily, that can be heard with greater joy, felt with more emotion or produced with greater effect.
—St. Augustine, *Letter 72*

We should not accept in silence the benefactions of God, but return thanks for them.
—St. Basil the Great

There is no one who, with a little bit of thought, cannot but discover many reasons for being grateful to God. . . . Once we have come to an appreciation of all he has given to us, we will have abundant cause to give thanks continually.
—St. Bernard of Clairvaux,
Sermon for the Sixth Sunday after Pentecost

Act!

Count your blessings! Write your own personal "litany of thanks."

Make a list of what you are grateful for and keep adding to it. Recount this list occasionally as you pray, thanking God for each of the particular benefits he has bestowed on you. You may find it helpful to use Psalm 103 as a model for your litany of thanks.

▶ In the Spotlight
"I Make Myself a Leper, to Gain All to Jesus Christ"

From a letter Blessed Joseph Damien de Veuster wrote to his brother, Father Pamphile, in 1873, about six months after arriving on Molokai, Hawaii:

God has deigned to choose your unworthy brother to assist the poor people attacked by that terrible malady, so often mentioned in the Gospel—leprosy. For the last ten years this plague has been spreading in the [Hawaiian] islands and at last the Government found itself obliged to isolate those affected with it. Shut up in a corner of the island of Molokai, between inaccessible cliffs and the sea, these unfortunate creatures are condemned to perpetual exile. Out of the *two thousand* in all who have been here, some *eight hundred* are still living, and among them is a certain number of Catholics. A priest was wanted; but here was a difficulty. For, as all communication was forbidden with the rest of the Islands, a priest who should be placed here must consider himself shut up with the lepers for the rest of his life; and Mgr. Maigret, our Vicar-Apostolic, declared that he should not impose this sacrifice on any of us. So, remembering that on the day of my profession I had already put myself under a funeral pall, I offered myself to his Lordship to meet, if he thought it well, this second death. Consequently, on May 11, a steamer landed me here, together with a batch of fifty lepers. . . .

This may give you some idea of my daily work. Picture to yourself a collection of huts with eight hundred lepers. No doctor; in fact, as there is no cure, there seems no place for a doctor's skill.

Every morning, then, after my Mass, which is followed by an instruction, I go to visit the sick, half of whom are Catholics. On entering each hut, I begin by offering to hear their confession. Those who refuse this spiritual help, are not, therefore, refused temporal assistance, which is given to all without distinction. Consequently, every one, with the exception of a very few bigoted heretics, look on me as a father. As for me, I make myself a leper, to gain all to Jesus Christ. . . .

I have baptized more than a hundred persons since my arrival. A good part of these died with the white robe of baptismal grace. I have also buried a large number. The average of deaths is at least one a day. Many are so destitute that there is nothing to defray their burial expenses. They are simply wrapped in a blanket. As far as my duties allow the time, I make coffins myself for these poor people. . . .
—Blessed Joseph Damien de Veuster

Damien later contracted leprosy and died of the disease, after having served on Molokai for sixteen years. His presence there made the world realize that those afflicted with leprosy were not "unclean outcasts," but vulnerable human beings whom God deeply loved and who were worthy of the same respect and dignity as everyone else. His life of sacrifice turned attention around the world to caring for these unfortunate men and women. Father Joseph Damien de Veuster was beatified by Pope John Paul II on June 4, 1995, and the state of Hawaii has honored Damien with a statue that stands in the United States Capitol.

Practical Pointers for Bible Discussion Groups

A Bible discussion group is another key that can help us unlock God's word. Participating in a discussion or study group—whether through a parish, a prayer group, or a neighborhood—offers us the opportunity to grow not only in our love for God's word but also in our love for one another. We don't have to be trained Scripture scholars to benefit from discussing and studying the Bible together. Bible-study groups provide environments in which we can worship and pray together and strengthen our relationships with other Christians. The following guidelines can help a group get started and run smoothly.

Getting Started

- Decide on a regular time and place to meet. Meeting on a regular basis allows the group to maintain continuity without losing momentum from the previous discussion.

- Set a time limit for each session. An hour and a half is a reasonable length of time in which to have a rewarding discussion on the material contained in each of the sessions in this guide. However, the group may find that a longer time is even more advantageous. If it is necessary to limit the meeting to an hour, select sections of the material that are of greatest interest to the group.

- Designate a moderator or facilitator to lead the discussions and keep the meetings on schedule. This person's role is to help preserve good group dynamics by keeping the discussion on track. He or she should help ensure that no one monopolizes the session and that each person—especially shy or quiet individuals—is offered an opportunity to speak. The group may want to ask members to take turns moderating the sessions.

- Provide enough copies of the study guide for each member of the group, and ask everyone to bring a Bible to the meetings. Each session's Scripture text and related passages for reflection are printed in full in the guides, but you will find that a Bible is helpful for looking up other passages and cross-references. The translation provided in this guide is the New Revised Standard Version (Catholic edition). You may also want to refer to other translations—for example, the New American Bible or the New Jerusalem Bible—to gain additional insights into the text.

- Try to stay faithful to your commitment and attend as many sessions as possible. Not only does regular participation provide coherence and consistency to the group discussions, it also demonstrates that members value one another and are committed to sharing their lives with one another.

Session Dynamics

- Read the material for each session in advance and take time to consider the questions and your answers to them. The single most important key to any successful Bible study is having everyone prepared to participate.

- As a courtesy to all members of your group, try to begin and end each session on schedule. Being prompt respects the other commitments of the members and allows enough time for discussion. If the group still has more to discuss at the end of the allotted time, consider continuing the discussion at the next meeting.

- Open the sessions with prayer. A different person could be responsible for leading the opening prayer at each session. The prayer could be a spontaneous one, a traditional prayer such as the Our Father, or one that relates to the topic of that particular meeting. The members of the group might also want to begin some of the meetings with a song or hymn. Whatever you choose, ask the Holy Spirit to guide your discussion and study of the Scripture text presented in that session.

- Contribute actively to the discussion. Let the members of the group get to know you, but try to stick to the topic, so that you won't divert the discussion from its purpose. And resist the temptation to monopolize the conversation, so that everyone will have an opportunity to learn from one another.

- Listen attentively to everyone in the group. Show respect for the other members and their contributions. Encourage, support, and affirm them as they share. Remember that many questions have more than one answer and that the experience of everyone in the group can be enriched by considering a variety of viewpoints.

- If you disagree with someone's observation or answer to a question, do so gently and respectfully, in a way that shows that you value the person who made the comment, and then explain your own point of view. For example, rather than say "You're wrong!" or "That's ridiculous!" try something like, "I think I see what you're getting at, but I think that Jesus was saying something different in this passage." Be careful to avoid sounding aggressive or argumentative. Then, watch to see how the subsequent discussion unfolds. Who knows? You may come away with a new and deeper perspective.

- Don't be afraid of pauses and reflective moments of silence during the session. People may need some time to think about a question before putting their thoughts into words.

- Maintain and respect confidentiality within the group. Safeguard the privacy and dignity of each member by not repeating what has been shared during the discussion session unless you have been given permission to do so. That way everyone will get the greatest benefit out of the group by feeling comfortable enough to share on a deep, personal level.

- End the session with prayer. Thank God for what you have learned through the discussion, and ask him to help you integrate it into your life.

The Lord blesses all our efforts to come closer to him. As you spend time preparing for and meeting with your small group, be confident in the knowledge that Christ will fill you with wisdom, insight, and grace and the ability to see him at work in your daily life.

Sources and Acknowledgments

Introduction

Page 15:
René Latourelle, *The Miracles of Jesus and the Theology of Miracles*, trans. Matthew J. O'Connell (Mahwah, NJ: Paulist Press, 1988), 239.

Session 1: The Miracle at Cana

Page 19:
François Mauriac, *Life of Jesus* (New York: David McKay Company, Inc., 1951), 29.

Page 20:
Jean Vanier, *Drawn into the Mystery of Jesus through the Gospel of John* (Mahwah, NJ: Paulist Press, 2004), 52.

Page 29:
Fulton J. Sheen, *Life of Christ* (New York: Image Books/Doubleday, 1990), 76–77.

Alphonsus Liguori, *Sunday Sermons*, 48, quoted in *The Navarre Bible: The Gospel of St. John*, with a commentary by the members of the Faculty of Theology of the University of Navarre (Blackrock, Ireland: Four Courts Press, 1995), 63.

Mother Teresa, *Love: A Fruit Always in Season—Daily Meditations by Mother Teresa of Calcutta*, ed. Dorothy S. Hunt (San Francisco: Ignatius Press, 1987), 54.

Pages 30–31:
In the Land I Have Shown You: The Stories of 16 Saints and Christian Heroes of North America, ed. Jeanne Kun (Ijamsville, MD: The Word Among Us Press, 2002), 68–69.

SESSION 2: THE HEALING OF THE PARALYZED MAN

Page 33:
Herman Hendrickx, *The Miracle Stories of the Synoptic Gospels,* (London: Geoffrey Chapman, 1987), 256.

Pages 37–38:
Cyril of Alexandria, *Commentary on Luke, Homily 12,* quoted in *Ancient Christian Commentary on Scripture: Luke,* ed. Arthur A. Just, Jr. (Downers Grove, IL: InterVarsity Press, 2003), 92. Copyright © 2003 by the Institute of Classical Christian Studies (ICCS), Thomas C. Oden and Arthur A. Just Jr. Used with permission of InterVarsity Press, P.O. Box 1400, Downers Grove, IL 60515. www.ivpress.com.

Page 38:
Peter Chrysologos, in *Sunday Sermons of the Great Fathers,* at www.orthodox.net/greatlent/sun02gl-gleanings.html.

Page 42:
God Forgives, Can I? ed. Angela M. Burrin (Ijamsville, MD: The Word Among Us Press, 2003), 9–10.

Page 43:
George Montague, *Mark: Good News for Hard Times* (Ann Arbor, MI: Servant Books, 1981), 32.

Maria Boulding, *Prayer: Our Journey Home* (Ann Arbor, MI: Servant Books, 1980), 65.

Session 3: The Stilling of the Storm at Sea

Page 45:
René Latourelle, *The Miracles of Jesus and the Theology of Miracles,* trans. Matthew J. O'Connell (Mahwah, NJ: Paulist Press, 1988), 103.

Page 46:
Erasmo Leiva-Merikakis, *Fire of Mercy, Heart of the Word: Meditations on the Gospel according to St. Matthew, Volume One* (San Francisco: Ignatius Press, 1996), 374.

Page 47:
Latourelle, 110.

Page 52:
The Navarre Bible: The Gospel of St. Matthew, with a commentary by the members of the Faculty of Theology of the University of Navarre (Blackrock, Ireland: Four Courts Press, 1993), 91.

Page 53:
Leiva-Merikakis, 363, 373.

George Montague, *Mark: Good News for Hard Times* (Ann Arbor, MI: Servant Books, 1981), 62.

Pages 56–57:
Ephrem the Syrian, *Commentary on Tatian's Diatessaron 6.25,* quoted in *Ancient Christian Commentary on Scripture: Luke,* ed. Arthur A. Just Jr. (Downers Grove, IL: InterVarsity Press, 2003), 137. Copyright © 2003 by the Institute of Classical Christian Studies (ICCS), Thomas C. Oden and Arthur A. Just Jr. Used with permission of InterVarsity Press, P.O. Box 1400, Downers Grove, IL 60515. www.ivpress.com.

Page 57:

John Chrysostom, *Commentary on St. John I,* quoted in *Ancient Christian Commentary on Scripture: Luke,* 137. Used with permission.

Session 4: The Raising of the Widow's Son

Page 59:

Alfred McBride, *The Kingdom and the Glory: Meditation and Commentary on the Gospel of Matthew* (Huntington, IN: Our Sunday Visitor, 1992), 65.

Page 61:

René Latourelle, *The Miracles of Jesus and the Theology of Miracles,* trans. Matthew J. O'Connell (Mahwah, NJ: Paulist Press, 1988), 194.

Page 63:

Ephrem the Syrian, *Commentary on Tatian's Diatessaron 6.23,* quoted in *Ancient Christian Commentary on Scripture: Luke,* ed. Arthur A. Just Jr. (Downers Grove, IL: InterVarsity Press, 2003), 117. Copyright © 2003 by the Institute of Classical Christian Studies (ICCS), Thomas C. Oden and Arthur A. Just Jr. Used with permission of InterVarsity Press, P.O. Box 1400, Downers Grove, IL 60515. www.ivpress.com.

Pages 63–64:

Augustine, *Sermon 98,* 2, quoted in *The Navarre Bible: The Gospel of St. Luke,* with a commentary by the members of the Faculty of Theology of the University of Navarre (Blackrock, Ireland: Four Courts Press, 1993), 105.

Page 64:
Cyril of Alexandria, *Commentary on Luke, Homily 36*, quoted in *Ancient Christian Commentary on Scripture: Luke*, 118. Used with permission.

Page 66:
Stephen Binz, *The Names of Jesus* (Mystic, CT: Twenty-Third Publications, 2004), 109.

Page 67:
Paulinus of Nola, quoted in Rosemary Ellen Guiley, *The Quotable Saint* (New York: Checkmark Books, 2002), 112.

Page 69:
Herman Hendrickx, *The Miracle Stories of the Synoptic Gospels*, (London: Geoffrey Chapman, 1987), 262.

Carroll Stuhlmueller, *The Gospel According to Luke*, 74, quoted in *The Jerome Biblical Commentary*, ed. Raymond Brown, Joseph Fitzmyer, and Roland Murphy (Englewood Cliffs, NJ: Prentice-Hall, Inc., 1968), 137.

Pages 70–71:
Josemaría Escrivá, *Christ Is Passing By*, quoted in *The Navarre Bible: The Gospel of St. Luke*, 104–105.

SESSION 5: THE MULTIPLICATION OF THE LOAVES AND FISH

Page 73:
Fulton J. Sheen, *Life of Christ* (New York: Image Books/Doubleday, 1990), 135.

Page 74:
François Mauriac, *Life of Jesus* (New York: David McKay Company, Inc., 1951), 100–101.

Pages 77–78:
Ambrose, *Exposition of the Gospel of Luke 6.86, 88,* quoted in *Ancient Christian Commentary on Scripture: Luke,* ed. Arthur A. Just Jr. (Downers Grove, IL: InterVarsity Press, 2003), 151. Copyright © 2003 by the Institute of Classical Christian Studies (ICCS), Thomas C. Oden and Arthur A. Just Jr. Used with permission of InterVarsity Press, P.O. Box 1400, Downers Grove, IL 60515. www.ivpress.com.

Page 78:
Cyril of Alexandria, *Commentary on Luke, Homily 48,* quoted in *Ancient Christian Commentary on Scripture: Luke,* 152. Used with permission.

Page 80:
Mother Teresa, *Jesus, the Word to Be Spoken: Prayers and Meditations for Every Day of the Year,* compiled by Brother Angelo Devananda (Ann Arbor, MI: Servant Books, 1986), 19.

Pages 83–84:
Francis Xavier Nguyen Van Thuan, *Testimony of Hope,* trans. Julia Mary Darrenkamp and Anne Eileen Heffernan (Boston: Pauline Books & Media, 2000), 131–133. English language copyright © 2000, Daughters of St. Paul. Used by permission of Pauline Books & Media, 50 St. Paul's Avenue, Boston, MA 02130. All rights reserved.

Page 85:
Francis of Assisi, quoted in Paul Thigpen, *A Dictionary of Quotes From the Saints* (Ann Arbor, MI: Servant Publications, 2001), 77.

John Vianney, quoted in Jill Haak Adels, *The Wisdom of the Saints: An Anthology* (New York: Oxford University Press, 1989), 82.

Francis de Sales, quoted in *The Wisdom of the Saints: An Anthology*, 81.

SESSION 6: THE HEALING OF THE TEN SUFFERING FROM LEPROSY

Page 87:
Marcel Gervais, Homily at Notre Dame Cathedral, Ottawa, 14 October 2001, www.ecclesia-ottawa.org/absp/abse141001.html.

Page 92:
Hannah Whitall Smith, *Daily He Leads Me: Inspirational Devotions for Every Day of the Year*, selected and adapted by Ann Spangler (Ann Arbor, MI: Servant Publications, 1985), 154.

Page 97:
Augustine, *Letter 72*, quoted in Francis Fernandez, *In Conversation with God—Volume Five* (London: Scepter Ltd., 1997), 222.

Basil the Great, quoted in Paul Thigpen, *A Dictionary of Quotes From the Saints* (Ann Arbor, MI: Servant Publications, 2001), 230.

Bernard of Clairvaux, *Sermon for the Sixth Sunday after Pentecost*, quoted in *In Conversation with God—Volume Five*, 224.

Pages 98–99:
Damien de Veuster, quoted in John Farrow, *Damien the Leper* (New York: Image Books/Doubleday, 1999), 142–145.

Also in The Word Among Us Keys to the Bible Series

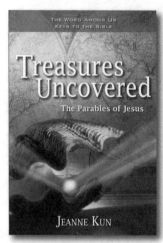

Item# BTWAE5

Treasures Uncovered
The Parables of Jesus
A Six-Week Bible Study for Catholics
by Jeanne Kun

The Good Samaritan, the Pearl of Great Price, the Lost Sheep—why did Jesus tell these stories, and what do they say to Christians today? This popular six-session Scripture guide will help readers explore the surprising—and often challenging—dimensions of six of Jesus' parables. Each chapter includes the full Scripture text of the parable, a short commentary, and questions that will help readers to deepen their understanding of the story and reflect on its meaning for their own lives. Short "In the Spotlight" sections supplement the commentary with fascinating historical details, explanations of the Greek root words used in the original gospels, and quotations from church fathers, saints, and contemporary Catholic writers. Readers will truly feel as if they have "uncovered" the treasures of the parables in this unique Catholic Scripture guide.